Introduction

Dear Food Lover,

Embark on a culinary journey where health meets taste, where every bite is a step towards wellbeing, and where the richness of flavors celebrates the joy of eating smart and living well. This isn't just a cookbook; it's your gateway to a lifestyle that cherishes the harmony between delicious meals and a healthy body.

In these pages, you will discover 100 meticulously crafted recipes that blend nutrition with mouth-watering tastes. From the comfort of hearty soups to the freshness of vibrant salads, the indulgence of decadent desserts to the wholesomeness of savory meats, we've covered all bases to ensure your meals are as enjoyable as they are nourishing.

Healthy and Delicious Foods

Learn the art of cooking meals that not only please your palate but also fuel your body with essential nutrients. Each recipe is a celebration of flavors that promises satisfaction without compromise.

Decadent Desserts

Who says healthy can't be indulgent? Our dessert section proves that you can enjoy the sweeter things in life without the guilt. These treats are not only a delight to your taste buds but are also kind to your health.

Vibrant Salads

Dive into the world of colorful salads that are as pleasing to the eye as they are to the palate. Packed with fresh ingredients and exciting dressings, these salads are perfect for any occasion, whether it's a light lunch or a side dish to complement your main course.

Soothing Soups

Discover the comfort of soups that warm the soul without weighing you down. From rich, creamy textures to light, brothy wonders, our soups are designed to satisfy and nourish.

Savory Meats

For those who love their meat but want to keep things healthy, our collection offers lean, flavor-packed recipes that make the most of high-quality proteins without the excess fats.

As you turn these pages, we invite you to cook, taste, and enjoy the journey towards a healthier, happier you. Whether you're a seasoned chef or a kitchen novice, these recipes are crafted to bring joy and health to every table.

Let the cooking begin!

© **Copyright 2024 - All rights reserved.**

You may not reproduce, duplicate or send the contents of this book without direct written permission from the author. You cannot hereby despite any circumstance blame the publisher or hold him or her to legal responsibility for any reparation, compensations, or monetary forfeiture owing to the information included herein, either in a direct or an indirect way.

Legal Notice: This book has copyright protection. You can use the book for personal purposes. You should not sell, use, alter, distribute, quote, take excerpts, or paraphrase in part or whole the material contained in this book without obtaining the permission of the author first.

Disclaimer Notice: You must take note that the information in this document is for casual reading and entertainment purposes only. We have made every attempt to provide accurate, up-to-date, and reliable information. We do not express or imply guarantees of any kind. The persons who read admit that the writer is not occupied in giving legal, financial, medical, or other advice. We put this book content by sourcing various places.

Please consult a licensed professional before you try any techniques shown in this book. By going through this document, the book lover comes to an agreement that under no situation is the author accountable for any forfeiture, direct or indirect, which they may incur because of the use of material contained in this document, including, but not limited to, a errors, omissions, or inaccuracies.

TABLE OF CONTENTS

1 BREAKFAST

Sunrise Berry Smoothie Bowl	5
Avocado Toast with Poached Egg	6
Quinoa Breakfast Porridge with Mixed Berries	7
Spinach and Feta Breakfast Wrap	8
Pumpkin Spice Overnight Oats	9
Egg Muffins with Spinach and Mushrooms	10
Banana Peanut Butter Chia Pudding	11
Sweet Potato and Black Bean Breakfast Burritos	12
Greek Yogurt Pancakes with Blueberry Compote	13
Savory Oatmeal with Avocado and Poached Egg	14
Almond Flour Waffles with Fresh Fruit	15
Zucchini and Carrot Fritters	16
Smoked Salmon and Cream Cheese Bagel	17
Vegan Tofu Scramble with Spinach and Tomatoes	18
Baked Avocado Eggs with Crispy Bacon	19
Cottage Cheese and Peach Parfait	20
Kale and Mushroom Savory Breakfast Bowl	21
Protein-Packed Smoothie with Spinach and Avocado	22
Whole Wheat Blueberry Muffins	23
Turmeric and Ginger Warm Breakfast Smoothie	24

2 SOUPS AND STEWS

Classic Chicken Noodle Soup	27
Hearty Beef and Vegetable Stew	28
Creamy Tomato Basil Soup	29
Rustic Lentil and Kale Stew	30
Spicy Thai Coconut Curry Soup	31
Minestrone with Seasonal Vegetables	32
Moroccan Chickpea and Sweet Potato Stew	33
Butternut Squash and Ginger Soup	34
French Onion Soup with Gruyère Toast	35
Tuscan White Bean and Kale Stew	36
Mexican Chicken Pozole Verde	37
New England Clam Chowder	38
Korean Spicy Tofu Stew	39
Italian Sausage and Tortellini Soup	40
West African Peanut Stew with Chicken	41

4 SALADS

Summer Berry Spinach Salad with Poppy Seed Dressing	43
Classic Caesar Salad with Homemade Croutons	44
Quinoa Tabbouleh with Fresh Herbs	45
Roasted Butternut Squash and Kale Salad	46
Avocado, Tomato, and Cucumber Salad with Lime Dressing	47
Mediterranean Chickpea Salad with Feta and Olives	48
Beetroot and Goat Cheese Salad with Walnuts	49
Asian-Style Slaw with Sesame Ginger Dressing	50
Grilled Peach and Burrata Salad with Balsamic Glaze	51
Southwestern Black Bean and Corn Salad	52
Caprese Salad with Balsamic Reduction	53
Crispy Chickpea and Sweet Potato Salad with Harissa Dressing	54
Watermelon, Feta, and Mint Salad with Honey Lime Vinaigrette	55
Shaved Brussels Sprouts Salad with Pecorino and Walnuts	56
Pear, Gorgonzola, and Candied Pecan Salad with Maple Balsamic Dressing	57

5 MEAT AND POULTRY

Garlic Butter Chicken Thighs 59
Honey Soy Baked Salmon 60
Lemon Herb Roasted Chicken 61
Easy Beef Stir-Fry with Vegetables 62
One-Pan Sausage and Vegetables 63
Spicy Lime Grilled Shrimp 64
Crockpot Pulled Pork 65
Turkey and Quinoa Stuffed Peppers 66
Balsamic Glazed Beef Steak 67
Maple Mustard Glazed Chicken 68
Simple Herb Roasted Turkey Breast 69
Quick Chicken Fajitas 70
Pork Chops with Apples and Onions 71
Beef and Broccoli 72
Chicken Parmesan in a Skillet 73
Bacon-Wrapped Dates with Goat Cheese 74
Greek Lemon Chicken Skewers 75
Sesame Ginger Salmon 76
Easy Chicken Piccata 77
Pan-Seared Duck Breast with Orange Sauce 78

6 FISH AND SEAFOOD

Lemon Butter Baked Cod Delight 80
Garlic Shrimp Zoodle Toss 81
Crispy Coconut Crusted Tilapia 82
Honey Glazed Salmon with Ginger 83
Simple Spicy Tuna Poke Bowl 84
Mediterranean Sea Bass en Papillote 85
Parmesan-Herb Crusted Haddock 86
Savory Shrimp and Grits Comfort 87
Clam and Chorizo Paella Fiesta 88
Sweet and Sour Grilled Mackerel 89

7 VEGETARIAN AND VEGAN

Creamy Avocado Spinach Pasta 91
Quinoa Stuffed Bell Peppers Delight 92
Hearty Lentil and Mushroom Stew 93
Chickpea Curry in a Hurry 94
Vegan Tofu Scramble Fiesta 95
Roasted Butternut Squash Soup 96
Zesty Black Bean and Corn Tacos 97
Sweet Potato and Kale Buddha Bowl 98
Eggplant Parmesan Magic 99
Crispy Cauliflower Buffalo Wings 100

8 SNACKS AND APPETIZERS

Garlicky Parmesan Zucchini Bites 102
Crisp Honey Sriracha Chicken Wings 103
Smoked Salmon Cucumber Rolls 104
Mini Caprese Skewers with Balsamic Glaze 105
Savory Spinach and Feta Puff Pastries 106
Sweet Potato Rounds with Goat Cheese and Cranberry 107
Baked Avocado Fries with Chipotle Aioli 108
Spicy Roasted Chickpeas 109
Prosciutto-Wrapped Asparagus Spears 110
Cheesy Garlic Breadsticks 111

9 DESSERTS

Decadent Chocolate Lava Cakes 113
Classic Vanilla Bean Panna Cotta 114
Easy Mixed Berry Crumble 115
No-Bake Lemon Cheesecake Cups 116
Fluffy Red Velvet Cupcakes 117
Cinnamon Apple Galette 118
Quick Chocolate Chip Cookie Bars 119
Peaches and Cream Tartlets 120
Coconut Mango Sticky Rice 121
Rustic Pear and Almond Tart 122

Breakfast

Think of breakfast as your day's jumpstart. It's not just about filling up; it's about setting the pace.

Whether it's a smoothie on the go or a sit-down stack of pancakes, the right morning meal can boost your energy, sharpen your focus, and keep those mid-morning cravings at bay. In this section, you'll find 20 recipes that do just that.

Quick, tasty, and nutritious, they're designed to fit into your morning rush and make sure you start your day off on the right foot. Let's make breakfast a priority and feel the difference it makes.

Sunrise Berry Smoothie Bowl

Ingredients:

- 1 cup mixed berries (strawberries, blueberries, raspberries, blackberries), fresh or frozen
- 1 banana, sliced
- 1/2 cup Greek yogurt (use plant-based for a vegan option)
- 1/4 cup almond milk (or any milk of your choice)
- 1 tablespoon honey or maple syrup (optional)
- Toppings: sliced fruits, chia seeds, homemade granola, coconut flakes, a drizzle of honey or maple syrup

Instructions:

Blend the Base: In a blender, combine the mixed berries, banana, Greek yogurt, almond milk, and honey/maple syrup (if using). Blend until smooth and creamy. Adjust the thickness by adding more milk if necessary.

Assemble Your Bowl: Pour the smoothie mixture into a bowl. Use a spatula or the back of a spoon to spread it out evenly.

Add Toppings: Creatively arrange your chosen toppings over the smoothie base. Mix textures and colors for an eye-catching and delicious finish.

Enjoy: Dive in with a spoon and enjoy every bite of your nutrient-packed, delicious smoothie bowl!

Chef's Note:

Feel free to customize your smoothie bowl with your favorite fruits and toppings. The key is to enjoy a balance of textures and nutrients that cater to your taste and dietary needs. This bowl is a canvas for your morning creativity!

Avocado Toast with Poached Egg

Ingredients:

- 2 slices of whole-grain bread
- 1 ripe avocado
- 2 eggs
- 1 tablespoon white vinegar (for poaching eggs)
- Salt and pepper, to taste
- Red pepper flakes (optional)
- Fresh herbs (such as cilantro or parsley), for garnish
- Extra-virgin olive oil, for drizzling

Instructions:

1. Prepare the Avocado: Cut the avocado in half, remove the pit, and scoop the flesh into a bowl. Mash the avocado with a fork until it's creamy but still has some chunks. Season with salt and pepper to taste.
2. Poach the Eggs: Fill a medium saucepan with about 3 inches of water and add the vinegar. Bring the water to a gentle simmer. Crack one egg into a small bowl. Stir the water in a circular motion with a spoon to create a whirlpool. Gently slide the egg into the center of the whirlpool. Repeat with the second egg. Cook for about 3-4 minutes for soft poached eggs, or until your desired doneness. Use a slotted spoon to remove the eggs from the water and set them on a paper towel to drain.
3. Toast the Bread: While the eggs are poaching, toast the bread slices to your preferred level of crispiness.
4. Assemble the Toast: Spread the mashed avocado evenly onto the toasted bread slices. Carefully place a poached egg on top of each avocado toast. Season with salt, pepper, and red pepper flakes (if using).
5. Garnish and Serve: Garnish with fresh herbs, drizzle with a bit of olive oil, and serve immediately.

Chef's Note:

Avocado toast with poached egg is a versatile recipe that you can customize according to your taste. Feel free to add toppings like smoked salmon, bacon, or tomatoes for extra flavor and nutrition. This dish combines the creaminess of avocado with the richness of a perfectly poached egg, making it a nutritious and satisfying breakfast option. Enjoy the simplicity of this meal, which is packed with healthy fats, protein, and fiber to start your day off right.

Quinoa Breakfast Porridge with Mixed Berries

Ingredients:

- 1 cup quinoa, rinsed and drained
- 2 cups almond milk, plus more for serving
- 1/2 teaspoon vanilla extract
- 1 tablespoon maple syrup, plus more for serving
- 1/2 teaspoon ground cinnamon
- A pinch of salt
- 1 cup mixed berries (such as strawberries, blueberries, raspberries)
- Optional toppings: sliced almonds, chia seeds, additional berries, a dollop of yogurt

Instructions:

1. **Cook Quinoa:** In a medium saucepan, combine the rinsed quinoa with 2 cups of almond milk, vanilla extract, maple syrup, ground cinnamon, and a pinch of salt. Stir to mix everything well.
2. **Simmer:** Bring the mixture to a boil over medium-high heat. Once boiling, reduce the heat to low, cover, and let it simmer for about 15 minutes, or until most of the liquid is absorbed and the quinoa is tender.
3. **Rest:** Remove the saucepan from the heat and let it sit, covered, for 5 minutes. This allows the quinoa to become fluffy and absorb any remaining liquid.
4. **Serve:** Fluff the quinoa with a fork and divide it among bowls. Top each serving with a generous amount of mixed berries. Add additional almond milk and maple syrup to taste. Sprinkle with your choice of toppings like sliced almonds, chia seeds, or a dollop of yogurt.

Chef's Note:

Quinoa breakfast porridge is a fantastic gluten-free alternative to traditional oatmeal, packed with protein and fiber to keep you full and energized throughout the morning. The beauty of this dish lies in its versatility; feel free to customize the toppings according to what's in season or your personal preference. Whether you're looking for a warm, comforting start to your day or a nutritious post-workout meal, this porridge delivers both taste and health benefits in every spoonful. Enjoy experimenting with different flavors and textures to make this breakfast uniquely yours.

Spinach and Feta Breakfast Wrap

Ingredients:

- 2 large eggs, beaten
- 1 tablespoon olive oil
- 2 cups fresh spinach leaves
- 2 whole wheat wraps or tortillas
- 1/4 cup feta cheese, crumbled
- Salt and pepper, to taste
- Optional: sliced tomatoes, avocado, or red onion for added flavor and crunch

Instructions:

1. Cook the Eggs: Heat a non-stick skillet over medium heat. Add the beaten eggs and scramble until fully cooked, about 2-3 minutes. Season with salt and pepper to taste. Remove from the skillet and set aside.
2. Sauté the Spinach: In the same skillet, heat the olive oil over medium heat. Add the spinach and sauté until just wilted, about 1-2 minutes. Season with a little salt and pepper.
3. Assemble the Wraps: Lay out the whole wheat wraps on a flat surface. Divide the scrambled eggs evenly between the two wraps, placing them in the center. Top with the sautéed spinach and crumbled feta cheese. If using, add sliced tomatoes, avocado, or red onion.
4. Wrap and Serve: Fold in the sides of the wrap and then roll it up tightly. Cut in half, if desired, and serve immediately.

Chef's Note:

This Spinach and Feta Breakfast Wrap is a delightful and nutritious way to start your day. The combination of tender scrambled eggs, wilted spinach, and tangy feta wrapped in a whole wheat tortilla offers a perfect balance of flavors and textures. It's a versatile recipe, so feel free to add other ingredients like tomatoes, avocado, or onions based on your preferences or what you have on hand. This wrap is not only easy to make but also portable, making it an excellent option for a quick breakfast on the go. Enjoy experimenting with this recipe and make it your own!

Pumpkin Spice Overnight Oats

Ingredients:

- 1/2 cup rolled oats
- 2/3 cup almond milk (or any milk of your choice)
- 1/4 cup pumpkin puree
- 1 tablespoon chia seeds
- 2 tablespoons maple syrup (adjust to taste)
- 1/2 teaspoon vanilla extract
- 1/2 teaspoon pumpkin pie spice
- A pinch of salt
- Optional toppings: chopped nuts (such as pecans or walnuts), a dollop of Greek yogurt, extra dash of pumpkin pie spice, or a drizzle of maple syrup

Instructions:

1. Mix Ingredients: In a mason jar or airtight container, combine the rolled oats, almond milk, pumpkin puree, chia seeds, maple syrup, vanilla extract, pumpkin pie spice, and a pinch of salt. Stir well to ensure everything is fully mixed.
2. Refrigerate: Seal the container with a lid and place it in the refrigerator overnight, or for at least 6 hours. This allows the oats to soak up the liquid and flavors, becoming soft and pudding-like.
3. Serve: The next morning, stir the oats well. If the mixture seems too thick, you can add a little more milk to reach your desired consistency.
4. Add Toppings: Top your overnight oats with your choice of nuts, a dollop of Greek yogurt, an extra sprinkle of pumpkin pie spice, or a drizzle of maple syrup for added flavor and texture.

Chef's Note:

Pumpkin Spice Overnight Oats are the epitome of fall flavors, making for a convenient and nutritious breakfast option. This recipe is incredibly versatile and forgiving, allowing you to adjust the sweetness or spice level to match your preferences. The addition of chia seeds not only thickens the oats but also adds a boost of fiber and omega-3 fatty acids, making this meal both hearty and healthy. Feel free to play around with the toppings to add crunch and creaminess, creating a breakfast that's as delightful to eat as it is easy to prepare.
Enjoy the taste of autumn in a jar!

Egg Muffins with Spinach and Mushrooms

Ingredients:

- 6 large eggs
- 1/2 cup milk (any kind)
- 1 cup fresh spinach, chopped
- 1/2 cup mushrooms, diced
- 1/4 cup onions, finely chopped
- 1/2 cup shredded cheese (cheddar, mozzarella, or your choice)
- Salt and pepper, to taste
- Cooking spray or oil, for greasing
- Optional: diced bell peppers, tomatoes, or cooked bacon for added flavor

Instructions:

1. **Preheat Oven and Prepare Pan:** Preheat your oven to 375°F (190°C). Grease a muffin tin with cooking spray or oil to prevent sticking.
2. **Sauté Vegetables:** In a skillet over medium heat, sauté the mushrooms and onions with a bit of oil until they are soft and lightly browned, about 5 minutes. Add the spinach and cook until just wilted. Remove from heat and let cool slightly.
3. **Mix Eggs:** In a large bowl, whisk together the eggs and milk. Season with salt and pepper. Stir in the cooled vegetable mixture and shredded cheese. If using, add any optional ingredients now.
4. **Fill Muffin Tin:** Evenly divide the egg mixture among the muffin cups, filling each about 3/4 full.
5. **Bake:** Place in the oven and bake for 20-25 minutes, or until the tops are set and lightly golden.
6. **Serve or Store:** Let the egg muffins cool for a few minutes before removing them from the tin. Serve immediately, or let them cool completely and store in the refrigerator for an easy grab-and-go breakfast.

Chef's Note:

Egg muffins are a versatile and convenient breakfast option, perfect for busy mornings or when you need a nutritious snack on the go. They're packed with protein and can be customized with your favorite veggies, cheeses, and add-ins. These muffins are also freezer-friendly; simply let them cool completely, then freeze on a baking sheet before transferring to a freezer-safe bag or container. Reheat in the microwave for a quick and satisfying meal. Enjoy experimenting with different combinations to find your favorite!

Banana Peanut Butter Chia Pudding

Ingredients:

- 1 large ripe banana, mashed
- 2 tablespoons peanut butter (smooth or crunchy)
- 1/2 cup chia seeds
- 2 cups almond milk (or any milk of your choice)
- 1 tablespoon maple syrup (optional, adjust to taste)
- 1/2 teaspoon vanilla extract
- A pinch of salt
- Optional toppings: sliced bananas, a dollop of peanut butter, chopped nuts, or chocolate chips

Instructions:

1. Combine Ingredients: In a mixing bowl, add the mashed banana and peanut butter. Mix until well combined. Add in the chia seeds, almond milk, maple syrup (if using), vanilla extract, and a pinch of salt. Stir thoroughly until everything is evenly mixed.
2. Refrigerate: Pour the mixture into a jar or an airtight container. Seal and refrigerate for at least 4 hours, or overnight, until the pudding has thickened and the chia seeds have absorbed the liquid, creating a gel-like consistency.
3. Serve: Once the pudding has set, give it a good stir to break up any clumps. Serve in bowls or glasses, topped with your choice of sliced bananas, a dollop of peanut butter, chopped nuts, or chocolate chips.

Chef's Note:

Banana Peanut Butter Chia Pudding is a deliciously easy and nutritious breakfast or snack option that combines the creamy sweetness of bananas with the rich, savory taste of peanut butter. This pudding is not only packed with fiber and omega-3 fatty acids from the chia seeds but also provides a good dose of protein and healthy fats, making it a satisfying meal to start your day or to enjoy as a midday snack. Feel free to customize the toppings according to your preferences or dietary needs. This pudding is best enjoyed chilled and can be stored in the refrigerator for up to 5 days, making it a convenient option for meal prep.

Sweet Potato and Black Bean Breakfast Burritos

Ingredients:

- 1 large sweet potato, peeled and diced into small cubes
- 1 can (15 oz) black beans, drained and rinsed
- 4 large eggs, beaten
- 4 whole wheat tortillas
- 1/2 cup shredded cheese (cheddar or Monterey Jack)
- 1 avocado, sliced
- 1/4 cup fresh cilantro, chopped
- 2 tablespoons olive oil
- 1 teaspoon ground cumin
- 1/2 teaspoon chili powder
- Salt and pepper, to taste
- Optional: salsa, sour cream, or hot sauce for serving

Instructions:

1. **Cook Sweet Potatoes:** In a large skillet, heat the olive oil over medium heat. Add the diced sweet potatoes, ground cumin, chili powder, salt, and pepper. Cook, stirring occasionally, until the potatoes are tender and lightly browned, about 10 minutes.
2. **Add Black Beans:** Stir in the black beans and cook for another 2-3 minutes until they are heated through. Remove the mixture from the skillet and set aside.
3. **Scramble Eggs:** In the same skillet, add the beaten eggs and scramble over medium heat until they are just set. Season with salt and pepper.
4. **Assemble Burritos:** Warm the tortillas according to package instructions. Divide the sweet potato and black bean mixture among the tortillas, followed by the scrambled eggs, shredded cheese, avocado slices, and fresh cilantro.
5. **Roll Burritos:** Fold in the sides of each tortilla and then roll them up tightly.
6. **Serve:** Serve the burritos immediately, with optional sides of salsa, sour cream, or hot sauce.

Chef's Note:

These Sweet Potato and Black Bean Breakfast Burritos are a hearty, nutritious way to start your day. The combination of sweet potatoes and black beans not only provides a good balance of complex carbohydrates and protein but also packs a flavorful punch thanks to the spices. Feel free to customize your burrito with additional toppings or condiments according to your taste. These burritos can also be made in advance, wrapped in foil, and refrigerated or frozen for a quick, on-the-go breakfast option. Just reheat in the oven or microwave when you're ready to enjoy!

Greek Yogurt Pancakes with Blueberry Compote

Ingredients:

- For the Pancakes:
- 1 cup all-purpose flour
- 2 tablespoons sugar
- 1 teaspoon baking powder
- 1/2 teaspoon baking soda
- 1/4 teaspoon salt
- 1 cup Greek yogurt
- 2 large eggs
- 1/2 teaspoon vanilla extract
- Butter or oil, for the pan
-
- For the Blueberry Compote:
- 2 cups fresh or frozen blueberries
- 1/4 cup water
- 2 tablespoons sugar
- 1 teaspoon lemon juice
- 1/2 teaspoon lemon zest

Instructions:

1. Make Blueberry Compote: In a small saucepan, combine blueberries, water, sugar, lemon juice, and lemon zest. Bring to a simmer over medium heat, stirring occasionally. Continue to cook for about 10 minutes, or until the berries have burst and the sauce has thickened slightly. Remove from heat and set aside to cool.
2. Prepare Pancake Batter: In a large bowl, whisk together flour, sugar, baking powder, baking soda, and salt. In another bowl, mix Greek yogurt, eggs, and vanilla extract until smooth. Add the wet ingredients to the dry ingredients, stirring until just combined; be careful not to overmix.
3. Cook Pancakes: Heat a non-stick skillet or griddle over medium heat and lightly grease with butter or oil. Pour 1/4 cup of batter for each pancake onto the skillet. Cook until bubbles form on the surface and the edges look set, about 2 minutes. Flip and cook for another 1-2 minutes or until golden brown and cooked through.
4. Serve: Serve the pancakes warm, topped with the blueberry compote.

Chef's Note:

These Greek Yogurt Pancakes with Blueberry Compote are a delightful twist on a classic breakfast. The Greek yogurt not only adds a tangy flavor but also ensures the pancakes are extra fluffy and moist. The homemade blueberry compote, with its balance of sweetness and acidity, perfectly complements the pancakes, making for a delicious and satisfying meal. This recipe can easily be doubled or tripled for larger gatherings, and the compote can be made ahead of time and stored in the refrigerator. Enjoy experimenting with different fruits for the compote to keep breakfast exciting!

Savory Oatmeal with Avocado and Poached Egg

Ingredients:

- 1 cup rolled oats
- 2 cups water or broth (for more flavor)
- 1 ripe avocado, sliced
- 2 eggs
- 1 tablespoon white vinegar (for poaching eggs)
- 2 tablespoons grated Parmesan cheese
- Salt and pepper, to taste
- Optional garnishes: chopped chives or green onions, red pepper flakes, a drizzle of olive oil

Instructions:

1. **Cook Oatmeal:** In a medium saucepan, bring the water or broth to a boil. Add the rolled oats and a pinch of salt, then reduce the heat to medium-low. Simmer, stirring occasionally, until the oats are soft and have absorbed the liquid, about 5 minutes. Remove from heat and stir in the grated Parmesan cheese. Adjust seasoning with salt and pepper to taste.
2. **Poach Eggs:** Fill a separate saucepan with about 3 inches of water and add the white vinegar. Bring to a simmer over medium heat. Crack an egg into a small bowl, then gently slide it into the simmering water. Repeat with the second egg. Cook for 3-4 minutes, until the egg whites are set but the yolks are still runny. Use a slotted spoon to remove the eggs from the water and drain them on a paper towel.
3. **Assemble:** Divide the cooked oatmeal between two bowls. Top each bowl with sliced avocado and a poached egg. Season with salt and pepper to taste.
4. **Garnish and Serve:** Add optional garnishes like chopped chives, red pepper flakes, or a drizzle of olive oil. Serve immediately.

Chef's Note:

Savory oatmeal is a delightful twist on the traditional breakfast staple, offering a heartier and more flavorful option to start your day. The combination of creamy avocado and a runny poached egg adds richness and depth, while the Parmesan infuses the oatmeal with a savory, umami kick. This dish is highly customizable; feel free to experiment with different broths, cheeses, or toppings to suit your taste. Not only is it nutritious—packed with fiber, healthy fats, and protein—but it's also a comforting and satisfying meal that's perfect for any time of day. Enjoy this modern take on oatmeal that bridges the gap between breakfast and brunch!

Almond Flour Waffles with Fresh Fruit

Ingredients:

- 2 cups almond flour
- 1 teaspoon baking powder
- 1/4 teaspoon salt
- 3 large eggs
- 1/4 cup unsweetened almond milk
- 2 tablespoons melted coconut oil or butter
- 1 tablespoon maple syrup (plus more for serving)
- 1 teaspoon vanilla extract
- Fresh fruit for topping (berries, sliced bananas, or your choice)
- Optional: whipped cream or yogurt for serving

Instructions:

1. **Mix Dry Ingredients:** In a large bowl, whisk together the almond flour, baking powder, and salt.
2. **Combine Wet Ingredients:** In another bowl, beat the eggs and then mix in the almond milk, melted coconut oil (or butter), maple syrup, and vanilla extract until well combined.
3. **Make Batter:** Pour the wet ingredients into the dry ingredients and stir until just combined. Be careful not to overmix; the batter should be slightly lumpy.
4. **Preheat Waffle Iron:** Heat your waffle iron according to the manufacturer's instructions. Lightly grease it with a bit of oil or spray to prevent sticking.
5. **Cook Waffles:** Pour the appropriate amount of batter onto the hot waffle iron (usually about 1/4 cup, but this can vary depending on your waffle iron). Close the lid and cook until the waffle is golden and crisp, usually about 3-5 minutes.
6. **Serve:** Serve the waffles hot, topped with fresh fruit and additional maple syrup. Add whipped cream or yogurt if desired.

Chef's Note:

These Almond Flour Waffles with Fresh Fruit offer a delightful, gluten-free alternative to traditional waffles, perfect for those looking for a low-carb or grain-free option. The almond flour not only provides a nutty flavor and tender texture but is also rich in nutrients. Topping these waffles with fresh fruit adds a burst of freshness and natural sweetness, making them a satisfying and wholesome breakfast or brunch option. Feel free to experiment with different fruits based on the season or your preference. Enjoy creating a beautiful and tasty start to your day with this healthy twist on a classic dish!

Zucchini and Carrot Fritters

Ingredients:

- 2 medium zucchinis, grated
- 2 medium carrots, grated
- 1/2 onion, finely chopped
- 2 cloves garlic, minced
- 2 large eggs, beaten
- 1/2 cup all-purpose flour (or almond flour for a gluten-free option)
- 1/4 cup grated Parmesan cheese
- 1 teaspoon salt
- 1/2 teaspoon black pepper
- 2 tablespoons fresh herbs (such as parsley or dill), chopped
- Olive oil, for frying

Instructions:

1. **Prepare Vegetables:** Place the grated zucchini and carrots in a colander, sprinkle with salt, and let sit for 10 minutes. Squeeze out as much liquid as possible to ensure the fritters are not soggy.
2. **Mix Ingredients:** In a large bowl, combine the drained zucchini and carrots with the onion, garlic, eggs, flour, Parmesan cheese, salt, pepper, and fresh herbs. Stir until well mixed.
3. **Heat Oil:** Heat a generous amount of olive oil in a large skillet over medium heat. The oil should cover the bottom of the skillet.
4. **Form and Fry Fritters:** For each fritter, spoon approximately 2 tablespoons of the mixture into the skillet, flattening with the back of the spoon to form a patty. Cook until golden brown and crispy, about 3-4 minutes per side. Work in batches to avoid overcrowding the pan.
5. **Drain:** Transfer the cooked fritters to a paper towel-lined plate to drain any excess oil.
6. **Serve:** Serve hot, accompanied by a dollop of sour cream, Greek yogurt, or your favorite dipping sauce.

Chef's Note:

Zucchini and Carrot Fritters are a versatile and delightful way to enjoy your vegetables. These fritters are crispy on the outside and tender on the inside, with a wonderful flavor from the Parmesan and fresh herbs. They make a great side dish, appetizer, or a light meal. The key to perfect fritters is draining the zucchini and carrots well to remove excess moisture. For a gluten-free version, you can substitute almond flour for the all-purpose flour. Feel free to experiment with additional veggies or spices to suit your taste. Enjoy these delicious and nutritious fritters with your favorite toppings or sauces!

Smoked Salmon and Cream Cheese Bagel

Ingredients:

- 2 bagels, halved and toasted
- 4 oz smoked salmon
- 4 tablespoons cream cheese
- 1/4 red onion, thinly sliced
- 1 tablespoon capers, drained
- Fresh dill, for garnish
- Freshly ground black pepper, to taste
- Optional: slices of tomato, cucumber, or avocado

Instructions:

1. Prepare Bagels: Start by toasting your bagel halves until they are golden and crispy to your liking.
2. Spread Cream Cheese: Spread a generous tablespoon of cream cheese on each toasted bagel half. The warmth of the bagel will help the cream cheese spread more easily.
3. Add Smoked Salmon: Layer slices of smoked salmon over the cream cheese on each bagel half. Depending on your preference, you can add more or less salmon.
4. Garnish: Add the thinly sliced red onion and capers on top of the smoked salmon. If using, add slices of tomato, cucumber, or avocado.
5. Season: Garnish with fresh dill and a sprinkle of freshly ground black pepper to taste.
6. Serve: Enjoy your Smoked Salmon and Cream Cheese Bagel immediately, accompanied by fresh fruit or a side salad for a complete meal.

Chef's Note:

This classic combination of smoked salmon and cream cheese on a bagel is not only delicious but also offers a good balance of protein, healthy fats, and carbohydrates. The creamy texture of the cream cheese pairs perfectly with the salty, smoky flavor of the salmon, while the capers and red onion add a punch of flavor and crunch. This dish is perfect for a luxurious breakfast, brunch, or even a light lunch. Feel free to customize your bagel with additional toppings like avocado for extra creaminess or cucumber for a refreshing crunch. Enjoy this gourmet treat any day of the week!

Vegan Tofu Scramble with Spinach and Tomatoes

Ingredients:

- 1 block (14 oz) firm tofu, drained and pressed
- 2 tablespoons olive oil
- 1/2 cup onion, diced
- 2 cloves garlic, minced
- 1 cup fresh spinach leaves
- 1/2 cup cherry tomatoes, halved
- 1/4 teaspoon turmeric (for color)
- 1/2 teaspoon ground cumin
- Salt and pepper, to taste
- Nutritional yeast (optional, for a cheesy flavor)
- Fresh herbs (such as parsley or cilantro), for garnish

Instructions:

1. **Crumble Tofu:** After pressing the tofu to remove excess water, crumble it into bite-sized pieces using your hands or a fork. Aim for a consistency similar to scrambled eggs.
2. **Cook Onion and Garlic:** Heat olive oil in a large skillet over medium heat. Add diced onion and minced garlic, sautéing until the onion is translucent and fragrant, about 3-5 minutes.
3. **Add Tofu and Spices:** Increase the heat to medium-high and add the crumbled tofu to the skillet. Sprinkle turmeric, ground cumin, salt, and pepper over the tofu. Stir well to evenly distribute the spices and cook for about 5-7 minutes, until the tofu is heated through and begins to get a slightly golden color.
4. **Add Vegetables:** Reduce the heat to medium. Add the fresh spinach and cherry tomatoes to the skillet, stirring gently until the spinach wilts and the tomatoes are just heated through, about 2-3 minutes.
5. **Final Seasoning:** Taste and adjust the seasoning as needed. If using, sprinkle nutritional yeast over the scramble for a cheesy flavor and added nutrients.
6. **Serve:** Remove from heat and garnish with fresh herbs before serving. Enjoy your tofu scramble on its own, or serve it alongside toast or in a wrap for a hearty meal.

Chef's Note:

This Vegan Tofu Scramble with Spinach and Tomatoes is a nutritious and flavorful alternative to traditional scrambled eggs. It's packed with protein, vitamins, and minerals, making it a perfect start to your day or a great addition to any meal. The turmeric not only adds a beautiful golden color but also provides anti-inflammatory benefits. Feel free to customize this versatile recipe by adding other vegetables or spices according to your preference. This scramble is a delightful way to enjoy a plant-based breakfast that's both satisfying and healthy.

Baked Avocado Eggs with Crispy Bacon

Ingredients:

- 2 ripe avocados
- 4 small eggs
- 4 strips of bacon
- Salt and pepper, to taste
- Chopped chives or parsley for garnish

Instructions:

1. **Preheat Oven and Prepare Bacon:** Preheat your oven to 425°F (220°C). Place the bacon strips on a baking sheet lined with parchment paper and bake until crispy, about 10-15 minutes depending on thickness. Once done, transfer to a paper towel-lined plate to drain and cool, then chop into small pieces.
2. **Prepare Avocados:** Cut the avocados in half and remove the pits. Use a spoon to scoop out a bit more avocado flesh to create enough space for an egg in each half.
3. **Crack Eggs:** Place the avocado halves on a baking tray. Carefully crack an egg into a small bowl, then slide it into the hollow of an avocado half. Repeat with the remaining eggs and avocado halves. Season with salt and pepper.
4. **Bake:** Bake in the preheated oven for 15-20 minutes, or until the eggs are cooked to your liking.
5. **Garnish and Serve:** Sprinkle the baked avocado eggs with crispy bacon pieces and chopped chives or parsley. Serve immediately.

Chef's Note:

Baked Avocado Eggs with Crispy Bacon combines the creamy texture of avocado with the rich taste of eggs and the salty crunch of bacon for a delightful breakfast or brunch dish. This recipe is not only simple to prepare but also packed with healthy fats, protein, and nutrients. Adjust the baking time based on how you prefer your eggs; less time for runny yolks, more for firm. For an extra kick, consider adding a sprinkle of cheese before baking or a dash of hot sauce before serving. Enjoy this deliciously balanced and satisfying meal to start your day off right!

Cottage Cheese and Peach Parfait

Ingredients:

- 1 cup cottage cheese
- 2 ripe peaches, sliced (or equivalent amount of canned peaches in juice, drained)
- 1/4 cup granola
- 2 tablespoons honey or maple syrup
- A pinch of cinnamon (optional)
- Fresh mint leaves for garnish (optional)

Instructions:

1. Layer the Parfait: Start by placing a layer of cottage cheese at the bottom of two glasses or parfait cups.
2. Add Peaches: Add a layer of sliced peaches on top of the cottage cheese. If you're using canned peaches, make sure they're well-drained to avoid making the parfait too watery.
3. Drizzle Sweetener: Lightly drizzle some honey or maple syrup over the peaches. If you like, sprinkle a pinch of cinnamon for added flavor.
4. Add Granola: Add a layer of granola on top of the peaches for a crunchy texture.
5. Repeat Layers: Repeat the layering process if your cups are tall enough, or if you prefer more layers, ending with a layer of peaches and a final drizzle of honey or maple syrup.
6. Garnish and Serve: Garnish with fresh mint leaves for a refreshing touch. Serve immediately or chill in the refrigerator for up to an hour before serving.

Chef's Note:

This Cottage Cheese and Peach Parfait is a delightful and healthy treat, perfect for breakfast or as a light dessert. The combination of creamy cottage cheese, sweet peaches, and crunchy granola offers a variety of textures and flavors that are sure to please. Cottage cheese is a great source of protein and calcium, making this parfait not only delicious but also nutritious. Feel free to substitute peaches with any seasonal fruits you have on hand, and adjust the sweetness to your liking. Enjoy this easy-to-make, refreshing parfait any time of the day!

Kale and Mushroom Savory Breakfast Bowl

Ingredients:

- 2 cups kale, stems removed and leaves chopped
- 1 cup mushrooms, sliced (any variety you prefer)
- 2 tablespoons olive oil
- 2 cloves garlic, minced
- 2 large eggs
- 1/4 cup quinoa (uncooked)
- 1/2 avocado, sliced
- Salt and pepper, to taste
- Optional garnishes: red pepper flakes, grated Parmesan cheese, or a drizzle of balsamic glaze

Instructions:

1. Cook Quinoa: Rinse the quinoa under cold water. In a small saucepan, bring 1/2 cup of water to a boil. Add the quinoa, cover, and reduce the heat to low. Simmer for about 15 minutes, or until the water is absorbed. Remove from heat and let it sit, covered, for 5 minutes. Fluff with a fork.
2. Sauté Kale and Mushrooms: While the quinoa is cooking, heat 1 tablespoon of olive oil in a large skillet over medium heat. Add the minced garlic and cook until fragrant, about 1 minute. Add the mushrooms and cook until they are soft and browned, about 5-7 minutes. Add the kale, season with salt and pepper, and cook until the kale is wilted and tender, about 3-4 minutes. Transfer to a plate and keep warm.
3. Fry Eggs: In the same skillet, add the remaining tablespoon of olive oil and fry the eggs to your liking. Season with salt and pepper.
4. Assemble Breakfast Bowl: Divide the cooked quinoa between two bowls. Top with the sautéed kale and mushrooms, fried egg, and sliced avocado.
5. Garnish and Serve: Add optional garnishes like red pepper flakes, grated Parmesan cheese, or a drizzle of balsamic glaze for extra flavor. Serve immediately.

Chef's Note:

This Kale and Mushroom Savory Breakfast Bowl is a hearty and nutritious way to start your day. Packed with protein, fiber, and healthy fats, it's designed to keep you satisfied until lunch. The combination of earthy mushrooms, tender kale, and creamy avocado offers a balance of textures and flavors that's both delicious and fulfilling. This breakfast bowl is highly customizable; feel free to add other vegetables or grains according to your preference. For a vegan option, skip the eggs or substitute them with tofu scramble. Enjoy this energizing and wholesome meal any morning!

Protein-Packed Smoothie with Spinach and Avocado

Ingredients:

- 1 cup fresh spinach leaves
- 1/2 ripe avocado
- 1 banana, sliced and frozen
- 1 scoop protein powder (vanilla or unflavored works best)
- 1 tablespoon chia seeds
- 1 cup almond milk (or any milk of your choice)
- 1/2 cup Greek yogurt (use plant-based yogurt for a vegan option)
- Ice cubes (optional, for a thicker smoothie)
- Honey or maple syrup to taste (optional, for sweetness)

Instructions:

1. Prepare Ingredients: Ensure your banana is sliced and frozen ahead of time for a creamy texture. Measure out all other ingredients.
2. Blend Smoothie: In a blender, combine the spinach, avocado, frozen banana, protein powder, chia seeds, almond milk, and Greek yogurt. If you're using ice cubes for a thicker smoothie, add them as well.
3. Adjust Sweetness: If desired, add honey or maple syrup to taste. This is optional and can be adjusted based on your preference for sweetness.
4. Blend Until Smooth: Blend on high speed until all the ingredients are thoroughly mixed and the smoothie has a creamy consistency.
5. Serve: Pour the smoothie into a glass and serve immediately. You can garnish with a sprinkle of chia seeds or a slice of avocado if desired.

Chef's Note:

This Protein-Packed Smoothie with Spinach and Avocado is a fantastic way to start your day or refuel after a workout. It's loaded with nutrients, healthy fats, and protein to keep you satisfied and energized. The combination of spinach and avocado provides a serving of vegetables and healthy fats, while the banana and yogurt add natural sweetness and creaminess. The protein powder and chia seeds boost the protein content, making it an ideal post-exercise recovery drink. You can customize this smoothie by adding other fruits or using different types of milk and yogurt to suit your dietary needs and preferences. Enjoy this delicious, healthful smoothie any time you need a quick and nutritious meal or snack!

Whole Wheat Blueberry Muffins

Ingredients:

- 2 cups whole wheat flour
- 1/2 cup sugar
- 1 tablespoon baking powder
- 1/2 teaspoon salt
- 1 cup fresh or frozen blueberries (if frozen, do not thaw)
- 1 egg
- 1 cup milk (any kind, dairy or non-dairy)
- 1/4 cup unsweetened applesauce
- 1/4 cup vegetable oil
- 1 teaspoon vanilla extract

Instructions:

1. **Preheat Oven and Prepare Pan:** Preheat your oven to 400°F (200°C). Line a muffin tin with paper liners or lightly grease the cups.
2. **Mix Dry Ingredients:** In a large bowl, whisk together the whole wheat flour, sugar, baking powder, and salt.
3. **Add Blueberries:** Gently fold the blueberries into the dry ingredients. This helps prevent the blueberries from sinking to the bottom of the muffins.
4. **Combine Wet Ingredients:** In a separate bowl, beat the egg lightly. Stir in the milk, applesauce, vegetable oil, and vanilla extract until well combined.
5. **Combine Wet and Dry Mixtures:** Pour the wet ingredients into the bowl with the dry ingredients and blueberries. Fold together with a spatula just until the dry ingredients are moistened. The batter will be lumpy; do not overmix.
6. **Fill Muffin Cups:** Spoon the batter into the prepared muffin cups, filling each about 3/4 full.
7. **Bake:** Bake for 20-25 minutes, or until a toothpick inserted into the center of a muffin comes out clean.
8. **Cool:** Allow the muffins to cool in the pan for 5 minutes, then transfer them to a wire rack to cool completely.

Chef's Note:

These Whole Wheat Blueberry Muffins are a healthier twist on a classic favorite, made with nutrient-rich whole wheat flour and packed with juicy blueberries. The addition of applesauce not only reduces the fat content but also keeps the muffins moist and tender. These muffins are perfect for a quick breakfast, a snack on the go, or a sweet treat any time of the day. Feel free to substitute the blueberries with other berries or diced fruit for variety. Enjoy these delicious muffins warm, with a pat of butter or a drizzle of honey for an extra special touch.

Turmeric and Ginger Warm Breakfast Smoothie

Ingredients:

- 1 cup almond milk (or your choice of milk)
- 1 banana, preferably ripe and sliced
- 1/2 teaspoon ground turmeric
- 1/2 teaspoon ground ginger
- 1/4 teaspoon cinnamon
- 1 tablespoon almond butter
- 1 teaspoon honey or maple syrup (adjust to taste)
- A pinch of black pepper (to enhance turmeric absorption)
- Optional: 1 scoop of your favorite protein powder

Instructions:

1. **Heat Milk:** Begin by gently heating the almond milk in a small saucepan over medium heat until it's warm but not boiling. Be careful not to overheat, as you don't want it too hot to drink.
2. **Blend Ingredients:** In a blender, combine the warm milk, sliced banana, turmeric, ginger, cinnamon, almond butter, honey (or maple syrup), and a pinch of black pepper. If you're adding protein powder, include it now.
3. **Blend Until Smooth:** Blend on high speed until the mixture is completely smooth. If the smoothie is too thick, you can add a little more warm milk to reach your desired consistency.
4. **Taste and Adjust:** Taste the smoothie and adjust the sweetness if needed by adding a bit more honey or maple syrup.
5. **Serve Warm:** Pour the smoothie into a mug or heat-resistant glass. Serve warm for a cozy start to your day.

Chef's Note:

This Turmeric and Ginger Warm Breakfast Smoothie offers a warming and nutritious way to start your morning, especially during the cooler months. Turmeric and ginger are well-known for their anti-inflammatory and antioxidant properties, making this smoothie not only delicious but also beneficial for your health. The addition of black pepper enhances the absorption of curcumin, the active compound in turmeric. This smoothie is a fantastic alternative for those who prefer a warm breakfast but still want the convenience and health benefits of a smoothie. Enjoy this comforting, spicy blend to kickstart your day with energy and warmth.

Soups and Stews

Soups and stews stand as the epitome of comfort food, offering warmth and nourishment across cultures and cuisines. These dishes, ranging from light and brothy to thick and hearty, embody the essence of home cooking, bringing together a medley of ingredients in a pot of simmering flavors.

Soups often serve as a soothing starter or a light meal, while stews provide a more robust and filling option, rich with the tastes of meats, vegetables, and spices that have melded together over slow cooking. Whether it's the simplicity of a clear vegetable soup or the complexity of a beef stew, these dishes are cherished for their ability to comfort, heal, and bring people together.

Perfect for any season, soups and stews are versatile dishes that can adapt to whatever is fresh and available, making them a staple in kitchens around the world.

Classic Chicken Noodle Soup

Ingredients:

- 2 tablespoons olive oil
- 1 cup diced onion
- 1 cup diced carrots
- 1 cup diced celery
- 2 garlic cloves, minced
- 8 cups chicken broth
- 2 bay leaves
- 1/2 teaspoon dried thyme
- Salt and pepper, to taste
- 2 cups cooked chicken, shredded (preferably breast or thigh)
- 2 cups egg noodles
- Fresh parsley, chopped, for garnish

Instructions:

1. Sauté the Vegetables: In a large pot, heat the olive oil over medium heat. Add the onion, carrots, and celery. Cook, stirring occasionally, until the vegetables are softened, about 5 minutes. Add the minced garlic and cook for another minute, until fragrant.
2. Add Broth and Seasonings: Pour in the chicken broth and add the bay leaves and dried thyme. Season with salt and pepper to taste. Bring the mixture to a boil, then reduce the heat to low and simmer for about 20 minutes to let the flavors meld.
3. Add Chicken and Noodles: Add the cooked, shredded chicken and egg noodles to the pot. Increase the heat to medium-high and let the soup come back to a gentle boil. Cook for 10 minutes, or until the noodles are tender.
4. Final Touches: Remove the bay leaves and adjust seasoning with more salt and pepper if needed.
5. Serve: Ladle the soup into bowls and garnish with chopped fresh parsley.

Chef's Note:

Classic Chicken Noodle Soup is the ultimate comfort food, perfect for chilly days or when you're in need of a warm, soothing meal. It's also great for using up leftover chicken. For a richer broth, you can use homemade chicken stock or add a piece of parmesan rind while it simmers. This soup is simple, yet full of flavor, and the fresh parsley at the end adds a nice touch of color and freshness. Enjoy it with some crusty bread for a complete meal.

Hearty Beef and Vegetable Stew

Ingredients:

- 2 pounds beef chuck, cut into 1-inch cubes
- Salt and pepper, to taste
- 2 tablespoons olive oil
- 1 large onion, chopped
- 3 cloves garlic, minced
- 3 carrots, peeled and sliced into 1/2-inch pieces
- 3 celery stalks, sliced into 1/2-inch pieces
- 2 tablespoons tomato paste
- 1 cup red wine (optional)
- 4 cups beef broth
- 2 bay leaves
- 1 teaspoon dried thyme
- 2 potatoes, peeled and cut into 1-inch cubes
- 1 cup frozen peas
- Fresh parsley, chopped, for garnish

Instructions:

1. **Brown the Beef:** Season the beef cubes with salt and pepper. In a large pot or Dutch oven, heat the olive oil over medium-high heat. Add the beef in batches, ensuring not to overcrowd the pan, and brown on all sides. Remove the beef and set aside.
2. **Sauté Vegetables:** In the same pot, add the onion, carrots, and celery. Cook over medium heat until the vegetables start to soften, about 5 minutes. Add the garlic and tomato paste, cooking for another minute until fragrant.
3. **Deglaze and Simmer:** Pour in the red wine (if using) to deglaze the pot, scraping up any browned bits from the bottom. Add the beef back to the pot along with the beef broth, bay leaves, and dried thyme. Bring to a boil, then reduce heat to low, cover, and simmer for 1 1/2 hours, or until the beef is tender.
4. **Add Potatoes and Finish Cooking:** Add the potatoes to the stew and continue to simmer, covered, for another 30 minutes, or until the potatoes are tender. In the last 5 minutes of cooking, stir in the frozen peas.
5. **Garnish and Serve:** Remove the bay leaves. Adjust the seasoning with more salt and pepper if needed. Serve the stew garnished with fresh parsley.

Chef's Note:

This Hearty Beef and Vegetable Stew is a classic comfort dish, perfect for colder months. The slow cooking process allows the flavors to meld beautifully, creating a rich, savory broth that complements the tender beef and vegetables. Feel free to customize the vegetables according to your preference or what's in season. For a thicker stew, you can remove a cup of the stew, mash the contents, and stir it back in before serving. Enjoy this hearty stew with crusty bread or over a bed of fluffy rice for a satisfying meal.

Creamy Tomato Basil Soup

Ingredients:

- 2 tablespoons olive oil
- 1 large onion, chopped
- 2 garlic cloves, minced
- 1 can (28 ounces) whole peeled tomatoes, in juice
- 2 cups vegetable broth
- 1/2 cup heavy cream (or coconut cream for a vegan option)
- 1/4 cup fresh basil leaves, plus more for garnish
- Salt and pepper, to taste
- Sugar, a pinch (optional, to balance acidity)
- Freshly grated Parmesan cheese (optional, for garnish)

Instructions:

1. Sauté Onion and Garlic: In a large pot, heat the olive oil over medium heat. Add the onion and cook until translucent, about 5 minutes. Add the minced garlic and cook for an additional minute, until fragrant.
2. Add Tomatoes and Broth: Pour in the whole peeled tomatoes, along with their juice, and the vegetable broth. Use a wooden spoon to break the tomatoes into smaller pieces. Bring the mixture to a boil, then reduce the heat and simmer for 20 minutes, allowing the flavors to meld.
3. Blend the Soup: Remove the pot from the heat. Using an immersion blender, blend the soup directly in the pot until smooth. Alternatively, you can use a regular blender, working in batches if necessary, to blend the soup until smooth. Return the soup to the pot if using a regular blender.
4. Add Cream and Basil: Stir in the heavy cream (or coconut cream) and fresh basil leaves. Return the pot to low heat and warm the soup gently, being careful not to let it boil. Season with salt, pepper, and a pinch of sugar (if using) to taste.
5. Serve: Ladle the soup into bowls. Garnish with additional fresh basil leaves and freshly grated Parmesan cheese (if using).

Chef's Note:

This Creamy Tomato Basil Soup is a classic comfort food, perfect for any season. The combination of ripe tomatoes and fresh basil creates a rich, flavorful base, while the addition of cream adds a luxurious texture. For a lighter version, you can substitute the heavy cream with half-and-half or even milk. This soup pairs wonderfully with a crusty piece of bread for dipping or a grilled cheese sandwich for a hearty meal. Enjoy the simplicity of this dish, where each spoonful warms you from the inside out.

Rustic Lentil and Kale Stew

Ingredients:

- 2 tablespoons olive oil
- 1 medium onion, diced
- 2 carrots, peeled and diced
- 2 celery stalks, diced
- 3 garlic cloves, minced
- 1 teaspoon ground cumin
- 1/2 teaspoon smoked paprika
- 1 cup dried green lentils, rinsed and drained
- 4 cups vegetable broth
- 1 can (14.5 ounces) diced tomatoes, with their juice
- 4 cups chopped kale, stems removed
- Salt and pepper, to taste
- Red pepper flakes, to taste (optional)
- Fresh lemon juice, for serving
- Grated Parmesan cheese (optional, for garnish)

Instructions:

1. Sauté the Vegetables: In a large pot, heat the olive oil over medium heat. Add the onion, carrots, and celery, cooking until the vegetables are softened, about 5 minutes. Add the minced garlic, cumin, and smoked paprika, and cook for another minute until fragrant.
2. Add Lentils and Broth: Stir in the green lentils, vegetable broth, and diced tomatoes (with their juice). Bring the mixture to a boil, then reduce the heat to low, cover, and simmer for about 25 minutes, or until the lentils are tender.
3. Incorporate Kale: Add the chopped kale to the pot, stirring until the kale is wilted and tender, about 5 minutes. Season with salt, pepper, and red pepper flakes (if using) to taste.
4. Finish and Serve: Remove the stew from the heat. Squeeze fresh lemon juice over the stew to enhance the flavors. Serve hot, garnished with grated Parmesan cheese (if using).

Chef's Note:

This Rustic Lentil and Kale Stew is a hearty, nutritious, and comforting meal, perfect for cold weather or anytime you're in need of some wholesome comfort food. The combination of earthy lentils, sweet vegetables, and bitter kale creates a symphony of flavors and textures that are both satisfying and healthy. The spices add a subtle warmth that complements the natural flavors of the ingredients. This stew is incredibly versatile; feel free to add other vegetables like sweet potatoes or squash to make it even more hearty. Enjoy it as is, or serve it with a slice of crusty bread for dipping.

Spicy Thai Coconut Curry Soup

Ingredients:

- 1 tablespoon coconut oil
- 1 small onion, finely chopped
- 2 garlic cloves, minced
- 1 tablespoon fresh ginger, grated
- 1 tablespoon Thai red curry paste
- 1 red bell pepper, sliced into thin strips
- 1 carrot, julienned
- 1 cup mushrooms, sliced
- 4 cups vegetable broth
- 1 can (14 ounces) coconut milk
- 1 tablespoon soy sauce
- 1 tablespoon sugar (optional, to balance flavors)
- 1 cup firm tofu, cubed
- 1 cup baby spinach leaves
- Juice of 1 lime
- Salt to taste
- Fresh cilantro and sliced red chili, for garnish

Instructions:

1. Sauté Aromatics: In a large pot, heat the coconut oil over medium heat. Add the onion, garlic, and ginger, sautéing until the onion is translucent and the mixture is fragrant, about 2-3 minutes.
2. Add Curry Paste and Vegetables: Stir in the Thai red curry paste until it's well combined with the aromatics. Add the red bell pepper, carrot, and mushrooms, cooking for another 5 minutes until the vegetables start to soften.
3. Simmer with Broth and Coconut Milk: Pour in the vegetable broth and coconut milk, bringing the mixture to a gentle simmer. Add the soy sauce and sugar (if using), and stir to combine. Allow the soup to simmer for about 10 minutes, letting the flavors meld together.
4. Add Tofu and Spinach: Add the cubed tofu and baby spinach to the pot. Continue to simmer until the spinach has wilted and the tofu is heated through, about 2-3 minutes. Stir in the lime juice and adjust the salt to taste.
5. Serve: Ladle the soup into bowls and garnish with fresh cilantro and slices of red chili for an extra kick.

Chef's Note:

This Spicy Thai Coconut Curry Soup is a vibrant, flavorful dish that brings a touch of Thai cuisine to your table. The combination of creamy coconut milk, spicy curry paste, and a variety of vegetables creates a deliciously complex flavor profile. The tofu adds a great source of protein, making this soup a satisfying meal on its own. Feel free to adjust the level of spice by adding more or less curry paste and chili according to your preference. This soup is best enjoyed fresh, but leftovers can be stored in the refrigerator and reheated, allowing the flavors to develop even further. Enjoy this warming, aromatic soup any time you're in need of a comforting, exotic escape.

Minestrone with Seasonal Vegetables

Ingredients:

- 2 tablespoons olive oil
- 1 large onion, diced
- 2 carrots, peeled and diced
- 2 celery stalks, diced
- 3 garlic cloves, minced
- 1 zucchini, diced
- 1 yellow squash, diced
- 1 cup green beans, trimmed and cut into 1-inch pieces
- 1 can (14.5 ounces) diced tomatoes, with their juice
- 6 cups vegetable broth
- 1 can (15 ounces) cannellini beans, drained and rinsed
- 1 cup small pasta (e.g., ditalini, orzo, or elbow macaroni)
- 1 teaspoon dried oregano
- 1 teaspoon dried basil
- Salt and pepper, to taste
- 2 cups baby spinach leaves
- Freshly grated Parmesan cheese, for serving
- Fresh basil, for garnish

Instructions:

1. **Sauté the Base Vegetables:** In a large pot, heat the olive oil over medium heat. Add the onion, carrots, and celery, cooking until the vegetables begin to soften, about 5 minutes. Add the garlic and cook for an additional minute until fragrant.
2. **Add Squash and Beans:** Stir in the zucchini, yellow squash, and green beans, cooking for another 5 minutes until they start to soften slightly.
3. **Simmer with Tomatoes and Broth:** Add the diced tomatoes (with their juice) and vegetable broth to the pot. Bring the mixture to a boil, then reduce the heat to a simmer. Stir in the cannellini beans, pasta, oregano, and basil. Season with salt and pepper to taste. Simmer for about 10-12 minutes, or until the pasta is cooked.
4. **Finish with Spinach:** Add the baby spinach to the pot, stirring until the spinach wilts, about 2 minutes.
5. **Serve:** Ladle the minestrone into bowls, and top with freshly grated Parmesan cheese and a sprinkle of fresh basil.

Chef's Note:

This Minestrone with Seasonal Vegetables is a hearty, nutritious soup that embodies the essence of Italian home cooking. It's versatile, allowing you to use whatever vegetables you have on hand or what's in season. The combination of beans, pasta, and a variety of vegetables makes it a filling meal perfect for any season. Feel free to swap out the vegetables based on availability or preference. For a richer flavor, you can add a parmesan rind to the soup while it simmers and remove it before serving. This minestrone is even more delicious the next day, as the flavors have more time to meld together. Serve with a side of crusty bread for a complete meal.

Moroccan Chickpea and Sweet Potato Stew

Ingredients:

- 2 tablespoons olive oil
- 1 large onion, diced
- 3 garlic cloves, minced
- 1 tablespoon grated ginger
- 1 tablespoon ground cumin
- 1 teaspoon ground cinnamon
- 1 teaspoon ground coriander
- 1/2 teaspoon cayenne pepper (adjust to taste for spiciness)
- 2 large sweet potatoes, peeled and cut into 1-inch cubes
- 1 can (15 ounces) chickpeas, drained and rinsed
- 1 can (14.5 ounces) diced tomatoes, with their juice
- 4 cups vegetable broth
- 1 teaspoon salt, or to taste
- 1/2 teaspoon black pepper
- 2 cups baby spinach leaves
- 1/2 cup chopped cilantro, plus more for garnish
- Juice of 1 lemon

Instructions:

1. Sauté Aromatics: In a large pot, heat the olive oil over medium heat. Add the onion and cook until softened, about 5 minutes. Add the garlic, ginger, cumin, cinnamon, coriander, and cayenne pepper. Cook for another 2 minutes, stirring frequently, until the spices are fragrant.
2. Add Sweet Potatoes and Chickpeas: Stir in the sweet potatoes, chickpeas, diced tomatoes (with their juice), and vegetable broth. Bring the mixture to a boil, then reduce the heat to low, cover, and simmer for about 20-25 minutes, or until the sweet potatoes are tender.
3. Finish with Spinach and Cilantro: Add the spinach and chopped cilantro to the pot. Cook until the spinach has wilted, about 2-3 minutes. Remove from heat and stir in the lemon juice. Season with salt and pepper to taste.
4. Serve: Ladle the stew into bowls and garnish with additional cilantro. Serve hot.

Chef's Note:

This Moroccan Chickpea and Sweet Potato Stew is a hearty, flavorful dish that combines the sweetness of sweet potatoes with the rich, warm spices typical of Moroccan cuisine. The chickpeas add a wonderful texture and protein, making this stew a satisfying meal on its own. The addition of fresh spinach and cilantro at the end brings a burst of color and freshness, while the lemon juice brightens the flavors. This stew is vegan and gluten-free, catering to a wide range of dietary needs. Serve it with couscous, rice, or a slice of crusty bread for a complete meal. Enjoy the comforting warmth and depth of flavors this stew offers, perfect for any season.

Butternut Squash and Ginger Soup

Ingredients:

- 2 tablespoons olive oil
- 1 medium onion, chopped
- 2 cloves garlic, minced
- 2 tablespoons fresh ginger, grated
- 1 medium butternut squash (about 2 pounds), peeled, seeded, and cubed
- 4 cups vegetable broth
- Salt and pepper, to taste
- 1 can (14 ounces) coconut milk
- Juice of 1 lime
- Fresh cilantro, for garnish
- Toasted pumpkin seeds, for garnish

Instructions:

1. Sauté Aromatics: In a large pot, heat the olive oil over medium heat. Add the onion and sauté until translucent, about 5 minutes. Add the garlic and ginger, cooking for another minute until fragrant.
2. Cook Butternut Squash: Add the cubed butternut squash to the pot, stirring to coat with the onion, garlic, and ginger. Pour in the vegetable broth, and season with salt and pepper. Bring to a boil, then reduce heat and simmer, covered, for about 20 minutes, or until the squash is tender.
3. Blend Soup: Use an immersion blender to puree the soup directly in the pot until smooth. Alternatively, you can transfer the mixture to a blender, working in batches if necessary, and blend until smooth. Return the soup to the pot if using a blender.
4. Add Coconut Milk and Lime: Stir in the coconut milk, reserving a few tablespoons for garnish if desired, and warm through without bringing it to a boil. Remove from heat and stir in the lime juice.
5. Serve: Ladle the soup into bowls. Drizzle with the reserved coconut milk, and garnish with fresh cilantro and toasted pumpkin seeds.

Chef's Note:

This Butternut Squash and Ginger Soup is a creamy, comforting dish perfect for chilly days. The ginger adds a warming, spicy note that complements the sweetness of the butternut squash, while the coconut milk brings a creamy texture and subtle flavor that ties everything together. The lime juice adds a bright, acidic touch to balance the flavors. This soup is not only delicious but also packed with nutrients. Serve it as a starter for a dinner party or enjoy it as a light, satisfying meal. The vibrant color and rich texture make it as pleasing to the eye as it is to the palate.

French Onion Soup with Gruyère Toast

Ingredients:

- 4 tablespoons unsalted butter
- 4 large onions, thinly sliced
- 2 garlic cloves, minced
- 1 teaspoon sugar
- 1/2 cup dry white wine
- 6 cups beef broth
- 1 bay leaf
- 1 teaspoon fresh thyme leaves (or 1/2 teaspoon dried thyme)
- Salt and freshly ground black pepper, to taste
- 1 baguette, sliced into 1-inch thick rounds
- 1 1/2 cups grated Gruyère cheese
- Fresh parsley, for garnish (optional)

Instructions:

1. Caramelize Onions: In a large pot, melt the butter over medium heat. Add the onions and cook, stirring occasionally, until they are deeply caramelized and golden brown, about 30-40 minutes. Add the garlic and sugar about halfway through to help with the caramelization and add depth of flavor.
2. Deglaze and Simmer: Add the white wine to the pot, scraping up any browned bits from the bottom. Cook until the wine has nearly evaporated. Add the beef broth, bay leaf, and thyme. Season with salt and pepper. Bring to a boil, then reduce heat and simmer for about 20 minutes to meld the flavors.
3. Prepare Gruyère Toasts: Preheat the broiler. Place the baguette slices on a baking sheet and toast under the broiler until lightly golden, about 1-2 minutes per side. Remove from the oven and sprinkle the toasted bread slices generously with grated Gruyère cheese. Return to under the broiler until the cheese is melted and bubbly, about 2-3 minutes.
4. Serve: Remove the bay leaf from the soup. Ladle the hot soup into bowls, and top each with a Gruyère toast. Garnish with fresh parsley if desired.

Chef's Note:

French Onion Soup with Gruyère Toast is a classic comfort dish known for its rich, savory flavors and luxurious cheese topping. The key to a great French onion soup is patience—allowing the onions to slowly caramelize brings out their natural sweetness, providing a robust foundation for the soup. The Gruyère cheese toasts add a delightful crunch and melty texture that pairs perfectly with the broth. This soup is ideal for a cozy night in or as an elegant starter for a dinner party. Enjoy the process and the delicious result of this timeless recipe.

Tuscan White Bean and Kale Stew

Ingredients:

- 2 tablespoons olive oil
- 1 large onion, diced
- 2 carrots, peeled and diced
- 2 celery stalks, diced
- 3 garlic cloves, minced
- 1 teaspoon dried rosemary
- 1 teaspoon dried thyme
- 1/2 teaspoon red pepper flakes (adjust to taste)
- 2 cans (15 ounces each) cannellini beans, drained and rinsed
- 4 cups vegetable broth
- 1 can (14.5 ounces) diced tomatoes, undrained
- 1 bunch kale, stems removed and leaves roughly chopped
- Salt and pepper, to taste
- Grated Parmesan cheese, for serving (optional)
- Fresh lemon wedges, for serving

Instructions:

1. **Sauté Aromatics:** In a large pot, heat the olive oil over medium heat. Add the onion, carrots, and celery, and cook until the vegetables begin to soften, about 5 minutes. Stir in the garlic, rosemary, thyme, and red pepper flakes, cooking for another minute until fragrant.
2. **Add Beans and Broth:** Add the cannellini beans, vegetable broth, and diced tomatoes (with their juice) to the pot. Bring the mixture to a simmer, then reduce the heat to low. Partially cover the pot and simmer for about 20 minutes, allowing the flavors to meld together.
3. **Incorporate Kale:** Stir in the chopped kale and continue to simmer until the kale is wilted and tender, about 5-10 minutes. Season with salt and pepper to taste.
4. **Serve:** Ladle the stew into bowls. If desired, top with grated Parmesan cheese and serve with fresh lemon wedges on the side.

Chef's Note:

This Tuscan White Bean and Kale Stew is a hearty, nutritious dish that brings the flavors of Italy into your kitchen. The combination of creamy cannellini beans and vibrant kale makes this stew both satisfying and packed with nutrients. The aromatic herbs and a hint of spice from the red pepper flakes add depth and warmth to the dish, making it a perfect meal for cooler weather. Serving the stew with Parmesan cheese adds a savory richness, while a squeeze of fresh lemon juice before eating brightens the flavors. This stew is wonderful on its own or served alongside crusty bread for dipping. Enjoy the simple, rustic elegance of this Tuscan-inspired stew any night of the week.

Mexican Chicken Pozole Verde

Ingredients:

- 1 tablespoon vegetable oil
- 1 large onion, chopped
- 3 cloves garlic, minced
- 2 pounds chicken breast, cut into bite-sized pieces
- Salt and pepper, to taste
- 6 cups chicken broth
- 2 cans (15 ounces each) hominy, drained and rinsed
- 1 pound tomatillos, husked and quartered
- 2 poblano peppers, seeded and chopped
- 1 jalapeño pepper, seeded and chopped (adjust to taste for heat)
- 1 cup fresh cilantro leaves, plus more for garnish
- Juice of 1 lime
- Radishes, sliced, for garnish
- Avocado, diced, for garnish
- Tortilla chips, for serving

Instructions:

1. Sauté Onion and Garlic: In a large pot, heat the vegetable oil over medium heat. Add the onion and garlic, and sauté until softened, about 5 minutes.
2. Brown the Chicken: Season the chicken pieces with salt and pepper, then add them to the pot. Cook until the chicken is browned on all sides, about 5-7 minutes.
3. Simmer with Broth and Hominy: Add the chicken broth and hominy to the pot. Bring to a simmer, cover, and cook for about 20 minutes, or until the chicken is cooked through.
4. Blend Tomatillos and Peppers: While the soup simmers, combine the tomatillos, poblano peppers, jalapeño pepper, and cilantro in a blender. Blend until smooth.
5. Combine and Cook: Add the blended tomatillo mixture to the pot. Stir well to combine and bring back to a simmer. Cook for an additional 10 minutes to meld the flavors. Stir in the lime juice and adjust seasoning with salt and pepper as needed.
6. Serve: Ladle the pozole into bowls and garnish with sliced radishes, diced avocado, and fresh cilantro leaves. Serve with tortilla chips on the side.

Chef's Note:

Mexican Chicken Pozole Verde is a vibrant and flavorful soup that's perfect for any occasion. The combination of tomatillos and poblano peppers creates a fresh, tangy sauce that complements the hearty hominy and tender chicken. This dish is a celebration of texture and taste, with each spoonful offering a burst of Mexican flavors. The garnishes of radish, avocado, and cilantro not only add a beautiful color contrast but also enhance the flavors and provide a refreshing crunch. Serve this comforting bowl of pozole with tortilla chips for dipping or crushing into the soup for extra texture. Enjoy this traditional dish as a satisfying main course that's sure to please a crowd.

New England Clam Chowder

Ingredients:

- 4 slices bacon, diced
- 1 large onion, chopped
- 2 celery stalks, diced
- 3 tablespoons all-purpose flour
- 2 cups chicken or vegetable broth
- 2 cups cubed potatoes (about 2 medium potatoes)
- 1 bay leaf
- 1 teaspoon dried thyme
- Salt and freshly ground black pepper, to taste
- 2 cans (6.5 ounces each) chopped clams in juice
- 1 cup heavy cream
- Fresh parsley, chopped, for garnish
- Oyster crackers, for serving

Instructions:

1. **Render Bacon:** In a large pot over medium heat, cook the diced bacon until crisp. Remove the bacon with a slotted spoon and set aside on a paper towel to drain, leaving the bacon fat in the pot.
2. **Sauté Vegetables:** Add the onion and celery to the pot with the bacon fat. Cook over medium heat until the vegetables are softened, about 5 minutes.
3. **Thicken with Flour:** Sprinkle the flour over the cooked vegetables, stirring well to combine. Cook for an additional minute to remove the raw flour taste.
4. **Add Broth and Potatoes:** Pour in the chicken or vegetable broth, then add the cubed potatoes, bay leaf, thyme, salt, and pepper. Bring the mixture to a boil, then reduce the heat and simmer until the potatoes are tender, about 10-15 minutes.
5. **Add Clams and Cream:** Stir in the clams with their juice and the heavy cream. Heat through, but do not boil, to avoid curdling the cream. Adjust seasoning with salt and pepper as needed.
6. **Serve:** Discard the bay leaf. Ladle the chowder into bowls and garnish with the cooked bacon pieces and chopped parsley. Serve with oyster crackers on the side.

Chef's Note:

New England Clam Chowder is a creamy, comforting soup that's a staple in American Northeastern cuisine. This version captures the essence of the sea with its tender clams and rich, creamy base, complemented by the smoky flavor of bacon and the earthiness of potatoes and celery. Remember to simmer gently after adding the cream to maintain the soup's smooth texture. Serving this chowder with oyster crackers adds a delightful crunch, enhancing the overall dining experience. Enjoy this hearty soup as a warm embrace on a chilly day, embodying the spirit of New England comfort food.

Korean Spicy Tofu Stew (Soondubu Jjigae)

Ingredients:

- 2 tablespoons sesame oil
- 2 tablespoons Korean red pepper flakes (gochugaru)
- 1 tablespoon minced garlic
- 1 teaspoon grated ginger
- 1 medium onion, thinly sliced
- 1 zucchini, cut into half-moons
- 4 cups vegetable or chicken broth
- 1 tablespoon soy sauce
- 1 tablespoon fish sauce (optional for depth of flavor)
- 1 block (14 ounces) soft tofu, cut into large cubes
- 8 ounces mushrooms, sliced (shiitake or button mushrooms)
- 1-2 green onions, chopped
- 1 teaspoon sesame seeds, for garnish
- 1 egg (optional), to be cracked into the stew just before serving

Instructions:

1. Prepare the Base: Heat the sesame oil in a large pot over medium heat. Add the Korean red pepper flakes, garlic, and ginger, stirring for about 1 minute until fragrant.
2. Add Vegetables: Add the onion and zucchini to the pot, sautéing until they start to soften, about 3-5 minutes.
3. Simmer with Broth: Pour in the broth, soy sauce, and fish sauce (if using). Bring the mixture to a boil, then reduce heat and simmer for about 10 minutes to develop the flavors.
4. Add Tofu and Mushrooms: Gently add the tofu and mushrooms to the pot. Return to a simmer and cook for an additional 5 minutes, being careful not to break up the tofu too much.
5. Final Touches: If using, crack an egg into the center of the stew just before serving. Do not stir; allow the egg to poach in the hot stew.
6. Serve: Ladle the stew into bowls, making sure to get a mix of tofu, vegetables, and broth. Garnish with chopped green onions and sesame seeds.

Chef's Note:

Soondubu Jjigae is a comforting, spicy Korean stew known for its deep, vibrant flavor and silky tofu. The key to this dish is the gochugaru, which provides its characteristic heat and red color. Adjust the amount of gochugaru to suit your taste for spiciness. The optional egg adds richness to the broth, gently poaching in the stew's heat. Serve with a bowl of steamed rice to balance the bold flavors. Enjoy this warming dish on a cold day or whenever you crave the hearty, satisfying flavors of Korean cuisine.

Italian Sausage and Tortellini Soup

Ingredients:

- 1 tablespoon olive oil
- 1 pound Italian sausage (sweet or spicy, based on preference), casings removed
- 1 medium onion, diced
- 2 garlic cloves, minced
- 2 carrots, peeled and diced
- 2 celery stalks, diced
- 1 zucchini, diced
- 4 cups chicken broth
- 1 can (14.5 ounces) diced tomatoes, with their juice
- 1 teaspoon dried oregano
- 1 teaspoon dried basil
- Salt and pepper, to taste
- 9 ounces cheese tortellini (fresh or frozen)
- 3 cups baby spinach, roughly chopped
- Grated Parmesan cheese, for serving

Instructions:

1. **Cook the Sausage:** In a large pot, heat the olive oil over medium heat. Add the Italian sausage, breaking it apart with a spoon. Cook until browned and no longer pink, about 5-7 minutes. Remove the sausage with a slotted spoon and set aside on a plate.
2. **Sauté Vegetables:** In the same pot, add the onion, garlic, carrots, and celery. Cook over medium heat until the vegetables begin to soften, about 5 minutes. Add the zucchini and cook for an additional 2 minutes.
3. **Combine Ingredients:** Return the cooked sausage to the pot. Add the chicken broth, diced tomatoes (with their juice), oregano, basil, salt, and pepper. Bring the mixture to a boil, then reduce the heat and simmer for about 10 minutes to blend the flavors.
4. **Add Tortellini:** Stir in the tortellini and continue to simmer until the tortellini are cooked through, about 5 minutes for fresh tortellini or according to package instructions for frozen.
5. **Finish with Spinach:** Add the chopped spinach to the pot, stirring until the spinach wilts, about 1-2 minutes.
6. **Serve:** Ladle the soup into bowls and top with grated Parmesan cheese.

Chef's Note:

This Italian Sausage and Tortellini Soup is a hearty, comforting dish perfect for a chilly evening. The combination of savory sausage, cheese-filled tortellini, and fresh vegetables creates a rich and satisfying meal. You can choose between sweet or spicy Italian sausage based on your flavor preference. The addition of spinach adds a pop of color and nutrition, making this soup a balanced option. Serve it with crusty bread for dipping into the flavorful broth. This soup is a wonderful way to enjoy the tastes of Italy in a single bowl, easily adaptable to your taste and perfect for sharing with family and friends.

West African Peanut Stew with Chicken

Ingredients:

- 2 tablespoons vegetable oil
- 1 pound chicken breasts, cut into bite-sized pieces
- Salt and pepper, to taste
- 1 medium onion, diced
- 2 garlic cloves, minced
- 1 tablespoon fresh ginger, grated
- 1 teaspoon ground cumin
- 1 teaspoon ground coriander
- 1/2 teaspoon cayenne pepper (adjust to taste)
- 3 cups chicken broth
- 1 can (14.5 ounces) diced tomatoes, with their juice
- 1 cup natural peanut butter (smooth or chunky based on preference)
- 2 sweet potatoes, peeled and cut into 1-inch cubes
- 4 cups chopped kale or spinach
- Juice of 1 lime
- Chopped fresh cilantro, for garnish
- Cooked rice, for serving

Instructions:

1. Brown the Chicken: Heat the vegetable oil in a large pot over medium-high heat. Season the chicken pieces with salt and pepper, then add to the pot and cook until browned on all sides. Remove the chicken and set aside.
2. Sauté Aromatics: In the same pot, add the onion, garlic, and ginger. Cook over medium heat until the onion is translucent, about 5 minutes. Stir in the cumin, coriander, and cayenne pepper, cooking for another minute until fragrant.
3. Simmer with Broth and Tomatoes: Return the chicken to the pot. Add the chicken broth and diced tomatoes with their juice. Bring to a simmer, then reduce heat to maintain a gentle simmer.
4. Add Peanut Butter and Sweet Potatoes: Stir in the peanut butter until well combined with the broth. Add the sweet potatoes, cover, and simmer for about 20 minutes, or until the sweet potatoes are tender.
5. Add Greens and Lime Juice: Stir in the kale or spinach, and cook until the greens are wilted and tender, about 5 minutes. Stir in the lime juice and adjust seasoning with additional salt, pepper, or cayenne pepper as needed.
6. Serve: Ladle the stew over cooked rice in bowls. Garnish with chopped cilantro.

Chef's Note:

West African Peanut Stew with Chicken is a rich, hearty dish that combines the nuttiness of peanut butter with the savory flavors of chicken and spices. The sweet potatoes add a subtle sweetness that complements the spicy, creamy broth, while the greens bring freshness and color to the dish. This stew is a wonderful example of the depth and complexity of West African cuisine, offering a balance of flavors that is both comforting and exotic. Serve it over rice to soak up the delicious sauce, and enjoy this nutritious, flavorful meal with family and friends.

Salads

Salads are not just about leafy greens; they're a vibrant mix of crisp vegetables, juicy fruits, and a myriad of textures and flavors that make eating a joyous occasion.

Diving into a salad is like taking a step towards wellness, with each ingredient offering its own set of benefits. From the fiber-rich greens that aid digestion to the antioxidants in bright vegetables and fruits that fight off free radicals, salads are a powerhouse of nutrients. They're a delightful way to keep your body nourished, your skin glowing, and your energy levels high.

Beyond their health benefits, salads are a testament to the beauty of fresh produce. There's something genuinely satisfying about combining the season's best offerings into a dish that's as beautiful to look at as it is delicious to eat.

Whether it's a simple green salad dressed in a zesty vinaigrette or a more elaborate concoction with grains and legumes, salads are a versatile and essential part of any diet.

Summer Berry Spinach Salad with Poppy Seed Dressing

Ingredients:

- **For the Salad:**
  - 6 cups fresh baby spinach leaves
  - 1 cup strawberries, hulled and sliced
  - 1 cup blueberries
  - 1/2 cup raspberries
  - 1/2 cup blackberries
  - 1/2 cup toasted pecans or almond slices
  - 1/2 cup crumbled feta or goat cheese
  - 1/4 red onion, thinly sliced (optional)

- **For the Poppy Seed Dressing:**
  - 1/3 cup olive oil
  - 1/4 cup apple cider vinegar
  - 2 tablespoons honey
  - 1 tablespoon poppy seeds
  - 1 teaspoon Dijon mustard
  - Salt and pepper, to taste

Instructions:

1. Prepare the Dressing: In a small bowl, whisk together olive oil, apple cider vinegar, honey, poppy seeds, Dijon mustard, salt, and pepper until well combined. Taste and adjust seasoning as needed. Set aside.
2. Assemble the Salad: In a large salad bowl, combine the baby spinach leaves, strawberries, blueberries, raspberries, blackberries, toasted pecans (or almond slices), crumbled feta (or goat cheese), and red onion slices if using.
3. Dress the Salad: Drizzle the prepared poppy seed dressing over the salad, tossing gently to ensure all the ingredients are evenly coated.
4. Serve: Serve the salad immediately, or keep it chilled until ready to serve.

Chef's Note:

This Summer Berry Spinach Salad with Poppy Seed Dressing is a vibrant, nutritious dish perfect for warm weather. The combination of sweet berries, creamy cheese, and crunchy nuts with the tangy and sweet poppy seed dressing creates a delightful mix of flavors and textures. It's an excellent side dish for summer picnics, barbecues, or a refreshing meal on its own. The dressing can be made ahead of time and stored in the refrigerator to let the flavors meld. Feel free to customize the salad by adding other seasonal fruits or using your favorite nuts and cheese to make this salad your own. Enjoy the burst of summer in every bite!

Classic Caesar Salad with Homemade Croutons

Ingredients:

- **For the Salad:**
- 2 heads romaine lettuce, washed, dried, and torn into bite-sized pieces
- 1/2 cup grated Parmesan cheese
- Anchovy fillets (optional, to taste)

- **For the Croutons:**
- 1/2 loaf of day-old bread, cut into 1-inch cubes
- 2 tablespoons olive oil
- 1/2 teaspoon garlic powder
- Salt and pepper, to taste

- **For the Dressing:**
- 1 garlic clove, minced
- 2 tablespoons fresh lemon juice
- 1 teaspoon Dijon mustard
- 1 teaspoon Worcestershire sauce
- 1/2 teaspoon anchovy paste (or 2 anchovy fillets, mashed)
- 1/3 cup olive oil
- 1/4 cup grated Parmesan cheese
- Salt and pepper, to taste
- 1 egg yolk (optional, for richness)

Instructions:

1. **Make the Croutons:** Preheat your oven to 375°F (190°C). In a bowl, toss the bread cubes with olive oil, garlic powder, salt, and pepper until evenly coated. Spread on a baking sheet and bake for 10-15 minutes, or until golden and crispy. Set aside to cool.
2. **Prepare the Dressing:** In a small bowl, whisk together the garlic, lemon juice, Dijon mustard, Worcestershire sauce, and anchovy paste. Slowly whisk in the olive oil until the dressing is emulsified. Stir in the Parmesan cheese, and season with salt and pepper. If using, whisk in the egg yolk until the dressing is creamy.
3. **Assemble the Salad:** In a large salad bowl, combine the romaine lettuce, croutons, and grated Parmesan cheese. Drizzle with the dressing and toss until the salad is evenly coated. Adjust seasoning with salt and pepper if necessary.
4. **Serve:** Garnish with anchovy fillets if desired. Serve immediately.

Chef's Note:

Classic Caesar Salad with Homemade Croutons is a timeless dish that combines the crispness of fresh romaine lettuce with the crunch of golden croutons and the creamy tang of Caesar dressing. Making your croutons and dressing from scratch elevates this salad, offering a depth of flavor and freshness that can't be matched by store-bought alternatives. The optional addition of anchovies and egg yolk in the dressing adds authenticity and richness to the salad, but can be adjusted based on personal preference. Enjoy this classic as a starter or add grilled chicken or shrimp to make it a hearty main course.

Quinoa Tabbouleh with Fresh Herbs

Ingredients:

- 1 cup quinoa, rinsed
- 2 cups water
- 1/4 cup olive oil
- Juice of 2 lemons
- 1 garlic clove, minced
- Salt and pepper, to taste
- 1 cup fresh parsley, finely chopped
- 1/2 cup fresh mint, finely chopped
- 3 green onions, thinly sliced
- 1 cucumber, diced
- 2 ripe tomatoes, diced
- 1/4 cup crumbled feta cheese (optional)

Instructions:

1. Cook Quinoa: In a medium saucepan, bring the quinoa and water to a boil. Reduce the heat to low, cover, and simmer for 15 minutes, or until the quinoa is tender and the water is absorbed. Remove from heat and let it sit covered for 5 minutes. Fluff with a fork and allow to cool to room temperature.
2. Prepare Dressing: In a small bowl, whisk together olive oil, lemon juice, minced garlic, salt, and pepper. Set aside.
3. Mix Salad: In a large bowl, combine the cooled quinoa, parsley, mint, green onions, cucumber, and tomatoes. Toss the salad with the dressing until evenly coated.
4. Serve: Adjust the seasoning with more salt and pepper if needed. Garnish with crumbled feta cheese if using. Serve chilled or at room temperature.

Chef's Note:

Quinoa Tabbouleh with Fresh Herbs is a refreshing, nutritious take on the traditional Middle Eastern salad. Quinoa, a protein-rich grain, serves as a gluten-free alternative to bulgur wheat, making this dish both hearty and healthy. The combination of fresh herbs, crisp vegetables, and tangy lemon dressing creates a vibrant mix of flavors and textures. This dish is perfect as a light lunch, a side dish, or a contribution to a potluck or picnic. For the best flavor, let the tabbouleh sit for a bit before serving to allow the quinoa to absorb the dressing and the flavors to meld. Enjoy this modern twist on a classic salad that's as delightful to eat as it is colorful to behold.

Roasted Butternut Squash and Kale Salad

Ingredients:

- **For the Salad:**
  - 1 medium butternut squash, peeled, seeded, and cubed
  - 2 tablespoons olive oil
  - Salt and pepper, to taste
  - 1 bunch kale, stems removed and leaves torn into bite-sized pieces
  - 1/2 cup dried cranberries
  - 1/2 cup pecans, roughly chopped
  - 1/2 cup feta cheese, crumbled

- **For the Dressing:**
  - 1/4 cup olive oil
  - 2 tablespoons apple cider vinegar
  - 1 tablespoon Dijon mustard
  - 1 tablespoon maple syrup
  - Salt and pepper, to taste

Instructions:

1. **Roast the Squash:** Preheat your oven to 400°F (200°C). Toss the cubed butternut squash with 2 tablespoons of olive oil, salt, and pepper. Spread in a single layer on a baking sheet and roast for 25-30 minutes, or until tender and golden, turning once halfway through. Allow to cool slightly.
2. **Prepare the Dressing:** In a small bowl, whisk together the olive oil, apple cider vinegar, Dijon mustard, maple syrup, salt, and pepper until well combined. Set aside.
3. **Assemble the Salad:** In a large salad bowl, combine the torn kale leaves with a bit of the dressing and massage gently with your hands to soften the kale. Add the roasted butternut squash, dried cranberries, pecans, and crumbled feta cheese to the bowl.
4. **Dress and Serve:** Drizzle the remaining dressing over the salad and toss gently to combine. Serve immediately or let it sit for a few minutes to allow the flavors to meld.

Chef's Note:

This Roasted Butternut Squash and Kale Salad is a hearty, flavorful dish perfect for the fall and winter months. Roasting the butternut squash brings out its natural sweetness, which complements the earthy kale, tangy cranberries, crunchy pecans, and creamy feta cheese beautifully. Massaging the kale with a bit of the dressing tenderizes the leaves, making them more palatable and easier to digest. The maple syrup in the dressing adds a subtle sweetness that ties all the flavors together. This salad can be served as a substantial side dish or a light main course, offering a delightful combination of textures and tastes that celebrate the season's best produce.

Avocado, Tomato, and Cucumber Salad with Lime Dressing

Ingredients:

- **For the Salad:**
  - 2 ripe avocados, peeled, pitted, and diced
  - 2 large tomatoes, diced
  - 1 English cucumber, diced
  - 1/4 red onion, thinly sliced
  - 1/4 cup fresh cilantro, chopped (optional)

- **For the Lime Dressing:**
  - Juice of 2 limes
  - 3 tablespoons olive oil
  - 1 garlic clove, minced
  - Salt and pepper, to taste
  - 1 teaspoon honey or agave syrup (optional, for sweetness)

Instructions:

1. Prepare the Dressing: In a small bowl, whisk together lime juice, olive oil, minced garlic, salt, pepper, and honey (or agave syrup) if using, until well combined. Taste and adjust seasoning as needed.
2. Combine Salad Ingredients: In a large salad bowl, combine diced avocados, tomatoes, cucumber, red onion, and cilantro. Gently toss to mix the ingredients.
3. Dress the Salad: Drizzle the lime dressing over the salad and gently toss again to coat all the ingredients evenly. Be careful not to mash the avocado pieces.
4. Serve: Serve immediately, or chill in the refrigerator for about 30 minutes before serving to allow the flavors to meld.

Chef's Note:

This Avocado, Tomato, and Cucumber Salad with Lime Dressing is a fresh, vibrant dish perfect for warm weather meals or as a healthy side dish. The creamy avocado, juicy tomatoes, and crisp cucumber create a delightful texture contrast, while the lime dressing adds a zesty, tangy flavor that brightens the entire salad. The optional cilantro adds a touch of freshness and color, but the salad is equally delicious without it. This salad is best enjoyed fresh to maintain the textures and vibrant flavors of the ingredients. It's a simple yet flavorful dish that's sure to be a hit at any table.

Mediterranean Chickpea Salad with Feta and Olives

Ingredients:

- **For the Salad:**
  - 2 cans (15 ounces each) chickpeas, drained and rinsed
  - 1 cup cherry tomatoes, halved
  - 1 cucumber, diced
  - 1/2 red onion, thinly sliced
  - 1/2 cup Kalamata olives, pitted and halved
  - 3/4 cup feta cheese, crumbled
  - 1/4 cup fresh parsley, chopped
  - 1/4 cup fresh mint, chopped (optional)

- **For the Dressing:**
  - 1/4 cup olive oil
  - 2 tablespoons lemon juice
  - 1 garlic clove, minced
  - 1 teaspoon dried oregano
  - Salt and pepper, to taste

Instructions:

1. Prepare the Dressing: In a small bowl, whisk together olive oil, lemon juice, minced garlic, dried oregano, salt, and pepper until well combined. Set aside to let the flavors meld.
2. Combine Salad Ingredients: In a large salad bowl, combine chickpeas, cherry tomatoes, cucumber, red onion, Kalamata olives, feta cheese, parsley, and mint (if using). Toss gently to mix.
3. Dress the Salad: Pour the prepared dressing over the salad ingredients. Toss again gently until everything is evenly coated with the dressing.
4. Serve: Allow the salad to sit for about 10 minutes before serving to let the flavors combine. Adjust seasoning with more salt and pepper if needed. Serve chilled or at room temperature.

Chef's Note:

This Mediterranean Chickpea Salad with Feta and Olives is a vibrant, flavorful dish that embodies the fresh and tangy tastes of the Mediterranean. It's a perfect side dish for a summer barbecue, a nutritious lunch option, or a light dinner. The combination of creamy chickpeas, crisp vegetables, salty feta, and briny olives offers a delightful variety of textures and flavors. The fresh herbs add a burst of freshness, while the lemony dressing brings all the components together. This salad is not only delicious but also packed with protein and fiber, making it both satisfying and healthy. Enjoy the essence of Mediterranean cuisine with this easy-to-make, refreshing salad.

Beetroot and Goat Cheese Salad with Walnuts

Ingredients:

- **For the Salad:**
- 4 medium beetroots, roasted, peeled, and sliced
- 1/2 cup walnuts, toasted and roughly chopped
- 4 ounces goat cheese, crumbled
- 4 cups mixed salad greens (arugula, spinach, and watercress work well)
- 1/4 red onion, thinly sliced (optional)
- Fresh herbs for garnish (such as parsley or dill)

- **For the Dressing:**
- 3 tablespoons olive oil
- 1 tablespoon balsamic vinegar
- 1 teaspoon Dijon mustard
- 1 teaspoon honey
- Salt and pepper, to taste

Instructions:

1. Prepare the Beetroots: Preheat your oven to 400°F (200°C). Wrap the beetroots in foil and roast for about 50-60 minutes, or until tender. Allow them to cool, then peel and slice.
2. Toast the Walnuts: Place the walnuts on a baking sheet and toast in the oven for 5-8 minutes, or until golden and fragrant. Let them cool, then roughly chop.
3. Mix the Dressing: In a small bowl, whisk together olive oil, balsamic vinegar, Dijon mustard, honey, salt, and pepper until well combined.
4. Assemble the Salad: In a large salad bowl, combine the mixed salad greens, sliced beetroots, toasted walnuts, crumbled goat cheese, and red onion.
5. Dress and Serve: Drizzle the dressing over the salad and toss gently to combine. Serve immediately.

Chef's Note:

Beetroot and Goat Cheese Salad with Walnuts is a classic combination that offers a wonderful blend of flavors and textures. The earthiness of the beetroots, the creamy tanginess of the goat cheese, the crunch of the walnuts, and the freshness of the greens create a harmonious and satisfying salad. This dish is not only beautiful to look at but also packed with nutrients. Roasting the beetroots enhances their natural sweetness, which pairs beautifully with the balsamic dressing. This salad makes an elegant starter or a light main course and is perfect for impressing guests or treating yourself to a gourmet salad at home. Enjoy the vibrant colors and rich flavors that make this salad a delightful culinary experience.

Asian-Style Slaw with Sesame Ginger Dressing

Ingredients:

- **For the Slaw:**
- 4 cups shredded cabbage (mix of green and red for color)
- 1 cup shredded carrots
- 1 bell pepper (red or yellow), thinly sliced
- 1/2 cup thinly sliced green onions
- 1/4 cup chopped cilantro
- 1 tablespoon sesame seeds (for garnish)

- **For the Sesame Ginger Dressing:**
- 1/4 cup soy sauce
- 2 tablespoons sesame oil
- 2 tablespoons rice vinegar
- 1 tablespoon honey or maple syrup
- 1 tablespoon freshly grated ginger
- 1 garlic clove, minced
- 1 teaspoon lime juice
- 1 teaspoon chili flakes (optional, for heat)

Instructions:

1. Prepare the Dressing: In a small bowl, whisk together soy sauce, sesame oil, rice vinegar, honey (or maple syrup), grated ginger, minced garlic, lime juice, and chili flakes (if using). Set aside to let the flavors meld.
2. Combine Slaw Ingredients: In a large salad bowl, combine the shredded cabbage, shredded carrots, thinly sliced bell pepper, sliced green onions, and chopped cilantro.
3. Dress the Slaw: Pour the prepared sesame ginger dressing over the slaw ingredients. Toss well to ensure all the vegetables are evenly coated with the dressing.
4. Garnish and Serve: Sprinkle sesame seeds over the top of the slaw before serving. Serve as a fresh side dish or top with grilled chicken or tofu for a complete meal.

Chef's Note:

This Asian-Style Slaw with Sesame Ginger Dressing is a vibrant, flavorful dish that's perfect for any occasion. The crunchy vegetables paired with the aromatic and tangy dressing offer a refreshing take on traditional slaw. The sesame ginger dressing, with its balance of umami, sweetness, and a hint of spice, complements the crispness of the vegetables beautifully. This slaw is not only a feast for the eyes but also packed with nutrients. It's a versatile side that pairs well with a variety of main dishes, especially grilled meats or fish. Enjoy this delightful salad that brings a touch of Asia to your dining table, combining healthful eating with bold flavors.

Grilled Peach and Burrata Salad with Balsamic Glaze

Ingredients:

- **For the Salad:**
- 4 ripe peaches, halved and pitted
- 1 tablespoon olive oil
- 8 ounces burrata cheese
- 4 cups mixed greens (such as arugula, spinach, or baby lettuce)
- 1/4 cup toasted almonds or pecans, roughly chopped
- Fresh basil leaves, for garnish

- **For the Balsamic Glaze:**
- 1/2 cup balsamic vinegar
- 2 tablespoons honey or sugar

Instructions:

1. Prepare the Balsamic Glaze: In a small saucepan, combine balsamic vinegar and honey (or sugar). Bring to a simmer over medium heat and cook until the mixture is reduced by half and has a syrupy consistency, about 10-15 minutes. Set aside to cool.
2. Grill the Peaches: Preheat grill to medium-high heat. Brush the peach halves with olive oil. Place the peaches on the grill, cut side down, and grill until charred and tender, about 4-5 minutes per side. Remove from the grill and let cool slightly.
3. Assemble the Salad: Arrange the mixed greens on a serving platter or individual plates. Tear the burrata cheese and scatter it over the greens. Add the grilled peach halves to the salad. Sprinkle with toasted almonds or pecans and garnish with fresh basil leaves.
4. Serve with Balsamic Glaze: Drizzle the balsamic glaze over the salad just before serving.

Chef's Note:

Grilled Peach and Burrata Salad with Balsamic Glaze is a delightful combination of sweet, smoky, creamy, and tangy flavors, making it a perfect summer dish. The warmth of the grilled peaches melts the burrata slightly, blending beautifully with the crispness of the greens and the crunch of the nuts. The balsamic glaze adds a rich, tangy sweetness that ties all the components together. This salad is not only a feast for the taste buds but also a visual treat, with its vibrant colors and elegant presentation. It makes an excellent starter or light meal that's sure to impress. Enjoy the best of summer's flavors with this refreshing and sophisticated salad.

Southwestern Black Bean and Corn Salad

Ingredients:

- **For the Salad:**
  - 2 cans (15 ounces each) black beans, drained and rinsed
  - 2 cups corn kernels (fresh, frozen and thawed, or canned and drained)
  - 1 red bell pepper, diced
  - 1 avocado, diced
  - 1/2 red onion, finely chopped
  - 1/2 cup fresh cilantro, chopped
  - 1 jalapeño, seeded and minced (optional)

- **For the Dressing:**
  - 1/4 cup olive oil
  - Juice of 2 limes
  - 2 tablespoons red wine vinegar
  - 1 teaspoon ground cumin
  - 1/2 teaspoon chili powder
  - Salt and pepper, to taste

Instructions:

1. Prepare the Dressing: In a small bowl, whisk together olive oil, lime juice, red wine vinegar, ground cumin, chili powder, salt, and pepper until well combined. Set aside.
2. Combine Salad Ingredients: In a large salad bowl, mix together black beans, corn, red bell pepper, avocado, red onion, cilantro, and jalapeño (if using).
3. Dress the Salad: Pour the prepared dressing over the salad ingredients. Toss gently to ensure everything is evenly coated with the dressing.
4. Chill and Serve: Let the salad chill in the refrigerator for at least 30 minutes before serving to allow the flavors to meld. Serve cold or at room temperature.

Chef's Note:

This Southwestern Black Bean and Corn Salad is a vibrant and flavorful dish that's perfect for picnics, potlucks, or as a refreshing side on warm days. It combines the hearty textures of black beans and corn with the freshness of avocado, red bell pepper, and cilantro, all brought together with a zesty and slightly spicy dressing. The addition of jalapeño offers a nice kick, but it can be adjusted or omitted based on your spice preference. This salad is not only delicious but also packed with nutrients, making it a healthy option for any meal. Enjoy the bold flavors and colors of the Southwest in this simple yet satisfying salad.

Caprese Salad with Balsamic Reduction

Ingredients:

- **For the Salad:**
  - 4 large ripe tomatoes, sliced
  - 8 ounces fresh mozzarella cheese, sliced
  - Fresh basil leaves
  - Salt and freshly ground black pepper, to taste
  - Extra virgin olive oil, for drizzling

- **For the Balsamic Reduction:**
  - 1 cup balsamic vinegar
  - 2 tablespoons honey or sugar (optional, to sweeten)

Instructions:

1. Prepare the Balsamic Reduction: In a small saucepan, combine balsamic vinegar and honey (or sugar) if using. Bring to a boil over medium-high heat, then reduce the heat to low and simmer for about 15-20 minutes, or until the vinegar has reduced by half and has a syrupy consistency. Allow it to cool; it will thicken further as it cools.
2. Assemble the Salad: On a large platter, alternately layer the tomato slices, mozzarella cheese slices, and fresh basil leaves. Overlap them for a visually appealing presentation.
3. Season and Drizzle: Season the salad with salt and freshly ground black pepper. Drizzle extra virgin olive oil over the top of the salad.
4. Serve with Balsamic Reduction: Just before serving, drizzle the balsamic reduction over the salad.

Chef's Note:

Caprese Salad with Balsamic Reduction is a classic Italian dish that embodies the simplicity and elegance of Italian cuisine. The combination of juicy tomatoes, creamy mozzarella, and aromatic basil, enhanced with the sweet and tangy balsamic reduction, creates a harmonious blend of flavors and textures. This salad is perfect as a starter, a side dish, or even a light meal on its own. It's best enjoyed with high-quality ingredients, as each element shines in this simple preparation. The balsamic reduction can be made in advance and stored in an airtight container in the refrigerator. Enjoy this timeless dish that celebrates the fresh tastes of summer.

Crispy Chickpea and Sweet Potato Salad with Harissa Dressing

Ingredients:

- **For the Salad:**
  - 2 medium sweet potatoes, peeled and cubed
  - 1 can (15 ounces) chickpeas, drained, rinsed, and patted dry
  - 2 tablespoons olive oil, divided
  - Salt and pepper, to taste
  - 1 teaspoon smoked paprika
  - 4 cups mixed salad greens (e.g., arugula, spinach, kale)
  - 1/2 red onion, thinly sliced
  - 1/4 cup feta cheese, crumbled
  - 1/4 cup toasted pumpkin seeds

- **For the Harissa Dressing:**
  - 3 tablespoons olive oil
  - 1 tablespoon harissa paste (adjust according to spice preference)
  - 2 tablespoons lemon juice
  - 1 garlic clove, minced
  - 1 teaspoon honey or maple syrup
  - Salt and pepper, to taste

Instructions:

1. **Roast Sweet Potatoes and Chickpeas:** Preheat your oven to 400°F (200°C). Toss the sweet potatoes and chickpeas with 1 tablespoon of olive oil, salt, pepper, and smoked paprika. Spread them out on a baking sheet in a single layer. Roast for 25-30 minutes, or until the sweet potatoes are tender and the chickpeas are crispy, stirring halfway through.
2. **Prepare the Harissa Dressing:** While the sweet potatoes and chickpeas are roasting, whisk together olive oil, harissa paste, lemon juice, minced garlic, honey (or maple syrup), salt, and pepper in a small bowl. Adjust the seasoning and spice level to your taste.
3. **Assemble the Salad:** In a large salad bowl, combine the mixed salad greens and red onion. Add the roasted sweet potatoes and chickpeas while they are still warm.
4. **Dress and Garnish the Salad:** Drizzle the harissa dressing over the salad and toss gently to combine. Top with crumbled feta cheese and toasted pumpkin seeds before serving.

Chef's Note:

This Crispy Chickpea and Sweet Potato Salad with Harissa Dressing offers a delightful combination of flavors and textures. The warmth of the roasted sweet potatoes and crispy chickpeas pairs perfectly with the spicy and tangy harissa dressing, while the feta cheese and pumpkin seeds add creaminess and crunch. This salad is not only packed with nutrients but also full of bold flavors that will satisfy your taste buds. It makes a hearty lunch or a vibrant side dish for dinner. The harissa dressing can be adjusted to suit your spice tolerance, making it a versatile addition to your recipe collection. Enjoy this colorful, flavorful salad that's as nourishing as it is delicious.

Watermelon, Feta, and Mint Salad with Honey Lime Vinaigrette

Ingredients:

- **For the Salad:**
  - 4 cups cubed watermelon
  - 1 cup crumbled feta cheese
  - 1/4 cup fresh mint leaves, roughly chopped or torn
  - 1/2 red onion, thinly sliced (optional)

- **For the Honey Lime Vinaigrette:**
  - 1/4 cup olive oil
  - 2 tablespoons lime juice
  - 1 tablespoon honey
  - Salt and pepper, to taste

Instructions:

1. Prepare the Vinaigrette: In a small bowl, whisk together olive oil, lime juice, honey, salt, and pepper until well combined. Adjust the seasoning according to taste. Set aside.
2. Assemble the Salad: In a large salad bowl, combine the cubed watermelon, crumbled feta cheese, and fresh mint leaves. If using, add the thinly sliced red onion.
3. Dress the Salad: Drizzle the honey lime vinaigrette over the salad. Toss gently to ensure the salad is evenly coated with the dressing.
4. Serve: Serve the salad immediately, or chill in the refrigerator for a short time before serving to enhance the flavors.

Chef's Note:

This Watermelon, Feta, and Mint Salad with Honey Lime Vinaigrette is a refreshing and vibrant dish perfect for hot summer days. The sweet juiciness of the watermelon pairs beautifully with the salty tanginess of the feta cheese and the fresh, aromatic mint leaves. The honey lime vinaigrette adds a zesty sweetness that ties all the flavors together. This salad is not only delicious but also visually appealing, making it a great addition to any picnic, barbecue, or summer gathering. For the best taste, use ripe, seedless watermelon and high-quality feta cheese. This dish is a delightful celebration of summer flavors, offering a light and nutritious option that's sure to please everyone.

Shaved Brussels Sprouts Salad with Pecorino and Walnuts

Ingredients:

- **For the Salad:**
  - 1 pound Brussels sprouts, trimmed
  - 1/2 cup shaved Pecorino cheese
  - 1/2 cup toasted walnuts, roughly chopped
  - 1/3 cup dried cranberries or cherries

- **For the Dressing:**
  - 1/4 cup extra virgin olive oil
  - 2 tablespoons apple cider vinegar
  - 1 tablespoon Dijon mustard
  - 1 tablespoon honey
  - Salt and pepper, to taste

Instructions:

1. **Shave the Brussels Sprouts:** Using a food processor with a slicing attachment, a mandoline, or a sharp knife, thinly shave the Brussels sprouts. Place the shaved sprouts in a large salad bowl.
2. **Toast the Walnuts:** Preheat your oven to 350°F (175°C). Spread the walnuts on a baking sheet and toast in the oven for 5-8 minutes, or until they are fragrant and slightly browned. Let them cool before chopping.
3. **Prepare the Dressing:** In a small bowl, whisk together the olive oil, apple cider vinegar, Dijon mustard, honey, salt, and pepper until well combined and emulsified.
4. **Assemble the Salad:** Add the shaved Pecorino cheese, toasted walnuts, and dried cranberries to the bowl with the shaved Brussels sprouts. Pour the dressing over the salad and toss well to ensure everything is evenly coated.
5. **Serve:** Adjust seasoning with additional salt and pepper if needed. Serve immediately, or let the salad sit for about 10 minutes to allow the flavors to meld together.

Chef's Note:

This Shaved Brussels Sprouts Salad with Pecorino and Walnuts is a crunchy, nutty, and flavorful dish that's perfect for any season. Shaving the Brussels sprouts creates a tender and more palatable texture, which pairs beautifully with the sharpness of the Pecorino cheese and the earthy crunch of the walnuts. The dried cranberries add a touch of sweetness that complements the tangy and slightly sweet dressing. This salad is a great way to enjoy Brussels sprouts in a raw, refreshing form. It makes an excellent side dish for holiday meals or a nutritious addition to your regular meal rotation. The combination of textures and flavors is sure to delight your taste buds.

Pear, Gorgonzola, and Candied Pecan Salad with Maple Balsamic Dressing

Ingredients:

- **For the Salad:**
  - 2 ripe pears, cored and sliced
  - 6 cups mixed salad greens (e.g., arugula, spinach, mixed baby greens)
  - 1/2 cup Gorgonzola cheese, crumbled
  - 1/2 cup candied pecans

- **For the Candied Pecans:**
  - 1/2 cup pecan halves
  - 2 tablespoons maple syrup
  - Pinch of salt

- **For the Maple Balsamic Dressing:**
  - 1/4 cup balsamic vinegar
  - 1/4 cup extra virgin olive oil
  - 2 tablespoons maple syrup
  - 1 teaspoon Dijon mustard
  - Salt and pepper, to taste

Instructions:

1. Candy the Pecans: Preheat the oven to 350°F (175°C). In a bowl, toss the pecan halves with maple syrup and a pinch of salt until well coated. Spread on a baking sheet lined with parchment paper. Bake for 10-15 minutes, stirring once, until they are toasted and glossy. Allow to cool.
2. Prepare the Dressing: In a small bowl, whisk together the balsamic vinegar, olive oil, maple syrup, Dijon mustard, salt, and pepper until the dressing is emulsified. Adjust seasoning to taste.
3. Assemble the Salad: In a large salad bowl, combine the mixed salad greens, sliced pears, crumbled Gorgonzola cheese, and candied pecans. Toss gently to combine.
4. Dress the Salad: Drizzle the maple balsamic dressing over the salad just before serving. Toss lightly to ensure the salad is evenly coated.
5. Serve: Divide the salad among plates and serve immediately.

Chef's Note:

This Pear, Gorgonzola, and Candied Pecan Salad with Maple Balsamic Dressing is a delightful blend of sweet, savory, and crunchy elements, making it a sophisticated addition to any meal. The ripe pears offer a sweet juiciness that complements the sharpness of the Gorgonzola cheese, while the candied pecans add a delightful crunch and maple sweetness. The maple balsamic dressing ties all the flavors together with its rich, tangy, and sweet profile. This salad is perfect for impressing guests or enjoying a gourmet experience at home. It's an elegant dish that showcases the harmony of flavors and textures, ideal for special occasions or as a luxurious everyday treat.

Meat and Poultry

Meat and poultry have always been known to be quality-protein sources accompanied by vitamins and minerals that are important to most diets. Meat constitutes beef, pork, lamb, and mutton, while poultry constitutes chicken, turkey, ducks, and geese.

They contain important nutrients such as iron, zinc, and B-vitamins but have the fat content differing with the kinds of cuts. The common ways of preparation include grilling, roasting, and stewing.

They are nutritious, but they are advised to be eaten moderately, while the processed kinds, on the other hand, present a risk to health. Sustainable and ethical sourcing is also of growing concern, caused both by environmental and ethical consideration.

A similar kind of approach, by making sensible choices, one can equalize the benefits and impacts of consuming meat and poultry.

Garlic Butter Chicken Thighs

Ingredients:

- 8 bone-in, skin-on chicken thighs
- Salt and pepper, to taste
- 1 tablespoon olive oil
- 3 tablespoons unsalted butter
- 6 cloves garlic, minced
- 1 teaspoon dried thyme
- 1 teaspoon dried rosemary
- 1/2 cup chicken broth
- Juice of 1 lemon
- Fresh parsley, chopped, for garnish

Instructions:

1. Preheat Oven: Preheat your oven to 400°F (200°C).
2. Season Chicken: Season the chicken thighs with salt and pepper on both sides.
3. Brown Chicken: In a large oven-proof skillet, heat the olive oil over medium-high heat. Add the chicken thighs, skin-side down, and cook until the skin is golden and crispy, about 6-7 minutes. Flip the chicken and cook for another 2-3 minutes. Remove chicken from the skillet and set aside.
4. Make Garlic Butter Sauce: In the same skillet, reduce heat to medium. Add the butter and garlic, cooking until the garlic is fragrant, about 1 minute. Stir in the dried thyme, rosemary, chicken broth, and lemon juice. Bring to a simmer.
5. Bake: Return the chicken thighs to the skillet, skin-side up. Transfer the skillet to the oven and bake for 25-30 minutes, or until the chicken is cooked through.
6. Garnish and Serve: Garnish with fresh parsley before serving. Spoon the garlic butter sauce over the chicken when serving.

Chef's Note:

Garlic Butter Chicken Thighs is a simple yet incredibly flavorful dish that combines the juicy richness of chicken thighs with the aromatic intensity of garlic and herbs. The skin crisps up beautifully in the oven, while the meat stays tender and moist. This dish is perfect for a comforting weeknight dinner and pairs wonderfully with a variety of sides, from roasted vegetables to mashed potatoes. The garlic butter sauce not only adds depth to the chicken but can also be used as a delicious gravy for your side dishes. Enjoy this easy-to-make, comforting meal that's sure to become a family favorite.

Honey Soy Baked Salmon

Ingredients:

- 4 salmon fillets (about 6 ounces each)
- Salt and pepper, to taste
- 3 tablespoons honey
- 2 tablespoons soy sauce
- 1 tablespoon olive oil
- 2 cloves garlic, minced
- 1 teaspoon fresh ginger, grated
- Juice of 1/2 lemon
- 1 tablespoon sesame seeds (for garnish)
- Fresh green onions, thinly sliced (for garnish)

Instructions:

1. Preheat Oven and Prepare Salmon: Preheat your oven to 375°F (190°C). Line a baking sheet with parchment paper. Place the salmon fillets on the prepared baking sheet and season with salt and pepper.
2. Make Honey Soy Glaze: In a small bowl, whisk together the honey, soy sauce, olive oil, minced garlic, grated ginger, and lemon juice until well combined.
3. Glaze Salmon: Brush the honey soy glaze generously over the top of each salmon fillet. Reserve some glaze for basting.
4. Bake: Place the salmon in the oven and bake for about 15-20 minutes, or until the salmon easily flakes with a fork. Baste with the reserved glaze halfway through baking.
5. Garnish and Serve: Once done, sprinkle the baked salmon with sesame seeds and garnish with sliced green onions. Serve immediately.

Chef's Note:

Honey Soy Baked Salmon is a deliciously simple and flavorful dish that's perfect for a quick weeknight dinner or a special occasion. The honey and soy sauce create a sweet and savory glaze that caramelizes beautifully in the oven, giving the salmon a delightful glaze and enhancing its natural flavors. The addition of garlic and ginger adds a depth of flavor that complements the richness of the salmon. Garnishing with sesame seeds and green onions not only adds a touch of elegance but also brings freshness and texture to the dish. This recipe is a great way to enjoy salmon, providing a healthy, satisfying meal that's both easy to prepare and packed with flavor.

Lemon Herb Roasted Chicken

Ingredients:

- 1 whole chicken (about 4 to 5 pounds)
- Salt and freshly ground black pepper, to taste
- 2 tablespoons olive oil
- 2 lemons, one sliced and one juiced
- 4 garlic cloves, minced
- 1 tablespoon fresh rosemary, chopped
- 1 tablespoon fresh thyme, chopped
- 1 tablespoon fresh parsley, chopped (plus more for garnish)
- 1/2 cup chicken broth

Instructions:

1. Preheat Oven and Prepare Chicken: Preheat your oven to 375°F (190°C). Rinse the chicken and pat dry with paper towels. Season the cavity and outside of the chicken generously with salt and pepper.
2. Season and Stuff Chicken: Rub the outside of the chicken with olive oil. In a small bowl, mix the minced garlic, rosemary, thyme, and parsley. Rub half of this herb mixture inside the chicken cavity. Stuff the cavity with sliced lemons. Truss the chicken legs and tuck the wing tips under the body.
3. Roast: Place the chicken breast-side up in a roasting pan. Sprinkle the remaining herb mixture over the chicken and pour lemon juice and chicken broth into the bottom of the pan. Roast for about 1 hour and 20 minutes, or until the juices run clear and a thermometer inserted into the thickest part of the thigh reads 165°F (74°C). Baste the chicken occasionally with the pan juices.
4. Rest and Serve: Let the chicken rest for 10 minutes before carving. Garnish with fresh parsley and serve with pan juices.

Chef's Note:

Lemon Herb Roasted Chicken is a classic dish that's perfect for a hearty family meal or a special occasion. The combination of fresh herbs and lemon infuses the chicken with a bright, aromatic flavor, while the olive oil and pan juices keep it moist and tender. Roasting the chicken with lemon slices inside the cavity adds an extra layer of citrusy fragrance that complements the herbs beautifully. This recipe highlights the simplicity of using fresh ingredients to elevate a traditional roast chicken into a flavorful, comforting dish that's sure to impress. Remember to baste the chicken as it roasts to ensure a golden, crispy skin and juicy interior.

Easy Beef Stir-Fry with Vegetables

Ingredients:

- 1 pound beef sirloin, thinly sliced against the grain
- 2 tablespoons soy sauce (divided)
- 1 tablespoon cornstarch
- 3 tablespoons vegetable oil (divided)
- 1 red bell pepper, sliced
- 1 green bell pepper, sliced
- 1 medium onion, sliced
- 2 carrots, julienned
- 2 garlic cloves, minced
- 1 tablespoon ginger, minced
- 1/2 cup broccoli florets
- 1/4 cup beef broth or water
- 2 tablespoons oyster sauce
- 1 tablespoon hoisin sauce
- Salt and pepper, to taste
- Sesame seeds and sliced green onions for garnish

Instructions:

1. **Marinate the Beef:** In a bowl, combine the thinly sliced beef with 1 tablespoon of soy sauce and cornstarch. Let it marinate for at least 15 minutes.
2. **Prep and Cook Vegetables:** Heat 1 tablespoon of vegetable oil in a large skillet or wok over medium-high heat. Add the bell peppers, onion, and carrots. Stir-fry for about 3-4 minutes until just tender but still crisp. Add the garlic, ginger, and broccoli, cooking for another 2 minutes. Remove the vegetables from the skillet and set aside.
3. **Cook the Beef:** In the same skillet, add the remaining 2 tablespoons of vegetable oil. Add the marinated beef and stir-fry until it is no longer pink, about 2-3 minutes.
4. **Combine and Finalize:** Return the cooked vegetables to the skillet with the beef. Add the beef broth, remaining soy sauce, oyster sauce, and hoisin sauce. Stir well to combine and cook for another 2 minutes until the sauce has thickened slightly. Season with salt and pepper to taste.
5. **Serve:** Garnish with sesame seeds and green onions. Serve hot with steamed rice or noodles.

Chef's Note:

This Easy Beef Stir-Fry with Vegetables is a quick and flavorful dish that's perfect for a busy weeknight meal. The key to a successful stir-fry is to have all your ingredients prepped and ready to go before you start cooking, as the cooking process is fast. Marinating the beef not only tenderizes it but also adds depth to the flavor. Feel free to swap out the vegetables based on what you have on hand or your preferences. This versatile dish is a great way to incorporate more vegetables into your meals while enjoying the savory flavors of beef and a delicious sauce.

One-Pan Sausage and Vegetables

Ingredients:

- 1 pound smoked sausage, sliced into rounds
- 2 bell peppers (any color), sliced
- 1 large onion, sliced
- 2 medium zucchinis, sliced
- 2 medium carrots, sliced
- 1 pound baby potatoes, halved or quartered depending on size
- 2 tablespoons olive oil
- 1 teaspoon garlic powder
- 1 teaspoon smoked paprika
- Salt and pepper, to taste
- Fresh herbs (such as thyme or rosemary), for garnish

Instructions:

1. Preheat Oven: Preheat your oven to 400°F (200°C).
2. Prepare Vegetables and Sausage: In a large mixing bowl, combine the sliced sausage, bell peppers, onion, zucchinis, carrots, and baby potatoes. Drizzle with olive oil, then season with garlic powder, smoked paprika, salt, and pepper. Toss until everything is well coated.
3. Arrange on Baking Sheet: Spread the sausage and vegetable mixture evenly on a large baking sheet. Ensure the ingredients are in a single layer for even cooking.
4. Bake: Place the baking sheet in the oven and bake for 25-30 minutes, stirring halfway through, until the vegetables are tender and the sausage is browned.
5. Garnish and Serve: Once cooked, remove from the oven and garnish with fresh herbs. Serve warm directly from the pan.

Chef's Note:

This One-Pan Sausage and Vegetables recipe is a simple, hearty meal that's perfect for busy weeknights. The combination of smoked sausage with a variety of vegetables creates a flavorful and satisfying dish with minimal effort. Using a single pan means quick prep and easy cleanup. Feel free to customize the vegetables based on what you have on hand or your preferences. This dish is versatile, nutritious, and packed with flavor, making it a family favorite. Enjoy the convenience of a delicious, one-pan meal that brings comfort and taste to your dinner table.

Spicy Lime Grilled Shrimp

Ingredients:

- 1 pound large shrimp, peeled and deveined
- 2 tablespoons olive oil
- Juice and zest of 2 limes
- 2 cloves garlic, minced
- 1 teaspoon chili powder
- 1/2 teaspoon cayenne pepper (adjust based on spice preference)
- 1/2 teaspoon paprika
- Salt and pepper, to taste
- Fresh cilantro, chopped, for garnish
- Lime wedges, for serving

Instructions:

1. Marinate Shrimp: In a large bowl, whisk together olive oil, lime juice and zest, minced garlic, chili powder, cayenne pepper, paprika, salt, and pepper. Add the shrimp to the bowl and toss to coat evenly. Cover and refrigerate for 30 minutes to marinate.
2. Preheat Grill: Preheat your grill to medium-high heat. If using wooden skewers, soak them in water for at least 20 minutes to prevent burning.
3. Skewer Shrimp: Thread the marinated shrimp onto skewers, leaving a small space between each shrimp for even cooking.
4. Grill Shrimp: Grill the shrimp skewers for 2-3 minutes on each side, or until the shrimp are pink and opaque.
5. Garnish and Serve: Remove the shrimp from the grill and transfer to a serving platter. Garnish with chopped cilantro and serve with lime wedges on the side.

Chef's Note:

Spicy Lime Grilled Shrimp is a zesty, flavorful dish that's perfect for a quick and easy summer meal. The combination of lime, garlic, and spices infuses the shrimp with a vibrant, tangy flavor with just the right amount of heat. Grilling adds a delicious smoky note that complements the shrimp's natural sweetness. This dish is incredibly versatile and can be served as an appetizer, a main course, or even added to salads, tacos, or pasta. The key to perfectly grilled shrimp is not to overcook them, as they can become tough and rubbery. Enjoy this delightful seafood dish that's sure to impress with its bold flavors and simple preparation.

Crockpot Pulled Pork

Ingredients:

- 4-5 pounds pork shoulder (also known as pork butt)
- 1 tablespoon salt
- 1 tablespoon ground black pepper
- 2 tablespoons brown sugar
- 1 tablespoon smoked paprika
- 1 teaspoon garlic powder
- 1 teaspoon onion powder
- 1/2 teaspoon cayenne pepper (optional for heat)
- 1 cup chicken broth or apple cider
- 1/2 cup barbecue sauce (plus more for serving)
- 2 tablespoons apple cider vinegar
- 2 cloves garlic, minced

Instructions:

1. Mix the Dry Rub: In a small bowl, combine the salt, black pepper, brown sugar, smoked paprika, garlic powder, onion powder, and cayenne pepper (if using). Mix well.
2. Season the Pork: Rub the spice mixture all over the pork shoulder, ensuring it's evenly coated.
3. Prepare the Crockpot: Place the seasoned pork shoulder into the crockpot. Pour in the chicken broth or apple cider, barbecue sauce, apple cider vinegar, and add the minced garlic around the pork.
4. Cook: Cover and cook on low for 8-10 hours, or on high for 5-6 hours, until the pork is very tender and falls apart easily.
5. Shred the Pork: Remove the pork from the crockpot and shred it using two forks. Discard any excess fat.
6. Finish with Sauce: Skim off any fat from the liquid left in the crockpot and adjust the seasoning if necessary. Return the shredded pork to the crockpot and stir it into the juices. If desired, add more barbecue sauce for extra flavor.
7. Serve: Serve the pulled pork on buns with additional barbecue sauce and your favorite coleslaw or side dishes.

Chef's Note:

Crockpot Pulled Pork is a hassle-free way to make a tender, flavorful dish that's perfect for sandwiches, tacos, or as a main course. The slow cooking process allows the pork to become incredibly tender and absorb the rich, smoky flavors of the spices and barbecue sauce. This method is ideal for feeding a crowd or meal prepping, as it requires minimal active time and yields plenty of delicious pork. The key to perfect pulled pork is patience; the longer it cooks, the more tender and flavorful it becomes. Enjoy the ease and deliciousness of this classic comfort food made in your crockpot.

Turkey and Quinoa Stuffed Peppers

Ingredients:

- 4 large bell peppers, halved and seeds removed
- 1 cup quinoa, cooked
- 1 pound ground turkey
- 1 tablespoon olive oil
- 1 small onion, diced
- 2 cloves garlic, minced
- 1 teaspoon cumin
- 1 teaspoon paprika
- 1/2 teaspoon chili powder
- Salt and pepper, to taste
- 1 cup tomato sauce
- 1/2 cup chicken or vegetable broth
- 1 cup shredded cheese (cheddar, mozzarella, or a blend)
- Fresh cilantro, for garnish

Instructions:

1. **Preheat Oven:** Preheat your oven to 375°F (190°C). Arrange the bell pepper halves in a baking dish, cut-side up.
2. **Cook Turkey Mixture:** Heat olive oil in a skillet over medium heat. Add the diced onion and cook until soft, about 5 minutes. Add the minced garlic, cumin, paprika, chili powder, salt, and pepper, and cook for another minute. Add the ground turkey and cook until browned, breaking it up with a spoon as it cooks. Stir in the cooked quinoa and tomato sauce, and cook for an additional 2-3 minutes.
3. **Stuff the Peppers:** Spoon the turkey and quinoa mixture evenly into the bell pepper halves. Pour the broth into the bottom of the baking dish (this helps to steam the peppers as they bake).
4. **Bake:** Cover the baking dish with aluminum foil and bake for 30 minutes. Remove the foil, top each pepper half with shredded cheese, and bake uncovered for an additional 10-15 minutes, or until the cheese is melted and bubbly.
5. **Garnish and Serve:** Let the stuffed peppers cool for a few minutes before serving. Garnish with fresh cilantro.

Chef's Note:

Turkey and Quinoa Stuffed Peppers is a nutritious and flavorful dish that combines lean protein, whole grains, and vegetables in one. This recipe is a great way to enjoy a balanced meal with a beautiful presentation. The spices add depth to the turkey and quinoa filling, while the cheese topping provides a deliciously melty finish. These stuffed peppers are perfect for a wholesome weeknight dinner or as a healthy option for meal prep. The recipe is versatile; feel free to add other vegetables or spices according to your preference. Enjoy this comforting, colorful dish that's as pleasing to the eye as it is to the palate.

Balsamic Glazed Beef Steak

Ingredients:

- 2 beef steaks (such as ribeye or sirloin), about 1-inch thick
- Salt and freshly ground black pepper, to taste
- 2 tablespoons olive oil
- 1/2 cup balsamic vinegar
- 2 tablespoons brown sugar
- 2 cloves garlic, minced
- 1 teaspoon fresh rosemary, finely chopped
- 1 tablespoon unsalted butter

Instructions:

1. Season the Steaks: Season both sides of the steaks generously with salt and pepper.
2. Sear the Steaks: Heat olive oil in a skillet over medium-high heat. Add the steaks and cook for 4-5 minutes on each side for medium-rare, or until they reach your desired level of doneness. Remove the steaks from the skillet and set aside to rest.
3. Prepare the Balsamic Glaze: In the same skillet, reduce the heat to medium. Add the balsamic vinegar, brown sugar, minced garlic, and rosemary. Simmer for 5-7 minutes, or until the mixture has reduced by half and thickened into a glaze. Remove from heat and whisk in the butter until smooth and glossy.
4. Glaze the Steaks: Return the steaks to the skillet and coat them in the balsamic glaze, turning them over to ensure they are well coated on all sides.
5. Serve: Transfer the glazed steaks to plates, spooning any remaining glaze over them. Serve immediately.

Chef's Note:

Balsamic Glazed Beef Steak is a luxurious and flavor-packed dish that combines the rich taste of beef with the sweet and tangy complexity of a balsamic reduction. The glaze, enhanced with garlic and rosemary, adds a gourmet touch to the steaks, making this recipe perfect for a special occasion or a romantic dinner at home. The key to a perfect glaze is to let it simmer until it thickens enough to coat the back of a spoon. This recipe is simple yet elegant, ensuring a restaurant-quality meal that's easy to prepare. Pair with a side of roasted vegetables or a simple salad for a complete, satisfying meal.

Maple Mustard Glazed Chicken

Ingredients:

- 4 boneless, skinless chicken breasts
- Salt and freshly ground black pepper, to taste
- 2 tablespoons olive oil
- 1/4 cup maple syrup
- 2 tablespoons Dijon mustard
- 1 tablespoon apple cider vinegar
- 1 clove garlic, minced
- 1 teaspoon fresh thyme leaves (or 1/2 teaspoon dried thyme)

Instructions:

1. **Preheat Oven:** Preheat your oven to 375°F (190°C).
2. **Season Chicken:** Season the chicken breasts with salt and pepper on both sides.
3. **Brown Chicken:** Heat olive oil in an oven-proof skillet over medium-high heat. Add the chicken breasts and sear until golden brown, about 3-4 minutes per side. Remove the chicken from the skillet and set aside.
4. **Make the Glaze:** In the same skillet, reduce heat to medium. Add maple syrup, Dijon mustard, apple cider vinegar, minced garlic, and thyme. Stir to combine and bring the mixture to a simmer.
5. **Glaze Chicken:** Return the chicken to the skillet, spooning the glaze over the breasts to coat them evenly.
6. **Bake:** Transfer the skillet to the oven and bake for 20-25 minutes, or until the chicken is cooked through and the glaze is caramelized.
7. **Serve:** Let the chicken rest for a few minutes before serving. Spoon extra glaze from the skillet over the chicken when plating.

Chef's Note:

Maple Mustard Glazed Chicken is a delightful dish that combines the sweet and rich flavors of maple syrup with the tangy kick of mustard, creating a perfectly balanced glaze. This recipe is simple yet elegant, making it suitable for both weeknight dinners and special occasions. The apple cider vinegar and garlic add depth to the glaze, while thyme provides a hint of earthiness. Cooking the chicken in the same skillet used for the glaze helps to infuse it with maximum flavor. This dish pairs beautifully with roasted vegetables or a fresh salad for a complete meal. Enjoy the succulent chicken with its glossy, flavorful glaze for a satisfying and tasty dining experience.

Simple Herb Roasted Turkey Breast

Ingredients:

- 1 bone-in, skin-on turkey breast (about 3-4 pounds)
- 2 tablespoons olive oil
- 1 tablespoon fresh rosemary, finely chopped
- 1 tablespoon fresh thyme, finely chopped
- 2 teaspoons fresh sage, finely chopped
- Salt and freshly ground black pepper, to taste
- 4 garlic cloves, minced
- 1/2 lemon, for juicing

Instructions:

1. Preheat Oven: Preheat your oven to 350°F (175°C).
2. Prepare Turkey Breast: Rinse the turkey breast and pat it dry with paper towels. Place it in a roasting pan.
3. Season: In a small bowl, mix together olive oil, rosemary, thyme, sage, minced garlic, salt, and pepper. Rub this herb mixture all over the turkey breast, making sure to get under the skin for maximum flavor.
4. Add Lemon: Squeeze the juice of half a lemon over the turkey breast for a hint of citrus.
5. Roast: Roast in the preheated oven for about 90 minutes, or until a meat thermometer inserted into the thickest part of the breast reads 165°F (74°C). Baste the turkey breast with its juices halfway through the cooking time.
6. Rest and Serve: Once cooked, remove the turkey breast from the oven and let it rest for 10-15 minutes before slicing. This allows the juices to redistribute throughout the meat, ensuring it's moist and flavorful.

Chef's Note:

This Simple Herb Roasted Turkey Breast recipe is a delightful way to enjoy turkey without the hassle of cooking a whole bird. The combination of fresh herbs and garlic creates a flavorful crust that complements the tender, juicy meat. Lemon juice adds a bright note that cuts through the richness of the turkey. This dish is perfect for a smaller holiday gathering or a family dinner any time of year. It's straightforward, delicious, and sure to impress your guests with its aromatic flavors and succulent texture. Pair with your favorite sides for a complete, festive meal.

Quick Chicken Fajitas

Ingredients:

- 2 boneless, skinless chicken breasts, thinly sliced
- 1 tablespoon olive oil
- 1 teaspoon chili powder
- 1 teaspoon cumin
- 1/2 teaspoon paprika
- Salt and pepper, to taste
- 1 red bell pepper, sliced
- 1 green bell pepper, sliced
- 1 onion, sliced
- 2 cloves garlic, minced
- Juice of 1 lime
- 6-8 flour tortillas, warmed
- Optional garnishes: sour cream, guacamole, salsa, shredded cheese, fresh cilantro

Instructions:

1. Season Chicken: In a bowl, combine the chicken slices with chili powder, cumin, paprika, salt, and pepper. Toss to coat evenly.
2. Cook Chicken: Heat olive oil in a large skillet over medium-high heat. Add the seasoned chicken and cook for 5-6 minutes, or until fully cooked. Remove chicken from the skillet and set aside.
3. Sauté Vegetables: In the same skillet, add a bit more olive oil if needed. Sauté the bell peppers, onion, and garlic for about 4-5 minutes, or until they are tender and slightly charred.
4. Combine: Return the cooked chicken to the skillet with the vegetables. Add lime juice and toss everything together. Cook for an additional 1-2 minutes.
5. Serve: Spoon the chicken and vegetable mixture onto warmed flour tortillas. Add any desired garnishes like sour cream, guacamole, salsa, shredded cheese, or fresh cilantro.

Chef's Note:

Quick Chicken Fajitas are a fast, flavorful, and versatile dish perfect for busy weeknights. This recipe simplifies traditional fajitas without compromising on the vibrant flavors that make them a favorite. Marinating the chicken in spices ensures each bite is packed with flavor, while the quick sauté of fresh vegetables adds crunch and color. Serving them with a variety of garnishes allows everyone to customize their fajita to their taste. This meal is not only delicious but also a fun and interactive way to bring everyone together at the dinner table. Enjoy the convenience and taste of homemade fajitas any night of the week!

Pork Chops with Apples and Onions

Ingredients:

- 4 bone-in pork chops, about 1-inch thick
- Salt and freshly ground black pepper, to taste
- 2 tablespoons olive oil
- 2 apples, cored and sliced (preferably a firm variety like Fuji or Granny Smith)
- 1 large onion, sliced
- 2 cloves garlic, minced
- 1 teaspoon fresh thyme leaves (or 1/2 teaspoon dried thyme)
- 1/2 cup apple cider or apple juice
- 1/2 cup chicken broth
- 2 tablespoons unsalted butter

Instructions:

1. Season Pork Chops: Season both sides of the pork chops with salt and pepper.
2. Brown Pork Chops: Heat olive oil in a large skillet over medium-high heat. Add the pork chops and cook until golden brown on both sides, about 3-4 minutes per side. Remove the pork chops from the skillet and set aside.
3. Sauté Apples and Onions: In the same skillet, add the sliced apples and onions. Cook over medium heat until the onions are soft and the apples have begun to brown, about 5-7 minutes. Add the minced garlic and thyme, cooking for an additional minute until fragrant.
4. Deglaze: Pour in the apple cider (or juice) and chicken broth. Stir to lift any browned bits from the bottom of the skillet.
5. Simmer: Return the pork chops to the skillet, nestling them into the apple and onion mixture. Cover and simmer over low heat for 10-15 minutes, or until the pork chops are cooked through.
6. Finish with Butter: Remove the skillet from heat. Transfer the pork chops to a serving plate. Stir the butter into the apple and onion mixture until melted and the sauce has thickened slightly.
7. Serve: Spoon the apples, onions, and sauce over the pork chops. Serve immediately.

Chef's Note:

Pork Chops with Apples and Onions is a classic dish that beautifully marries the savory flavor of pork with the sweet and tangy notes of apples and cider. This recipe offers a comforting meal that's perfect for a cozy dinner at home. The key to this dish is to use a firm apple variety that holds up well during cooking, adding a delightful contrast to the tender pork chops. The thyme adds an earthy flavor that complements the sweetness of the apples and onions. This dish is a testament to the simplicity and elegance of combining traditional flavors, creating a satisfying and hearty meal that's sure to please any palate.

Beef and Broccoli

Ingredients:

- 1 pound flank steak, thinly sliced against the grain
- 1 tablespoon cornstarch
- 2 tablespoons vegetable oil, divided
- 4 cups broccoli florets
- 1/2 cup beef broth
- 1/4 cup soy sauce
- 2 tablespoons brown sugar
- 3 cloves garlic, minced
- 1 tablespoon fresh ginger, minced
- 2 teaspoons sesame oil
- 1 teaspoon chili flakes (optional for heat)
- Sesame seeds, for garnish
- Sliced green onions, for garnish

Instructions:

1. **Prepare the Beef:** Toss the thinly sliced flank steak with cornstarch until well coated. This helps to tenderize the beef and thicken the sauce later on.
2. **Cook the Beef:** Heat 1 tablespoon of vegetable oil in a large skillet or wok over medium-high heat. Add the beef in batches, searing quickly on both sides, just until browned. Remove the beef from the skillet and set aside.
3. **Sauté the Broccoli:** In the same skillet, add the remaining tablespoon of vegetable oil. Add the broccoli florets and stir-fry for about 3-4 minutes until they are bright green and tender-crisp. Remove from the skillet and set aside with the beef.
4. **Make the Sauce:** In the same skillet, add beef broth, soy sauce, brown sugar, garlic, ginger, sesame oil, and chili flakes (if using). Bring to a simmer, stirring frequently, until the sauce slightly thickens.
5. **Combine and Cook:** Return the beef and broccoli to the skillet, tossing everything together to coat well in the sauce. Cook for an additional 2-3 minutes, ensuring the beef is cooked through and the broccoli is heated.
6. **Garnish and Serve:** Sprinkle sesame seeds and sliced green onions over the top. Serve hot with steamed rice or noodles.

Chef's Note:

Beef and Broccoli is a classic Chinese-American dish that's beloved for its savory, slightly sweet sauce and the tender-crisp contrast between the beef and broccoli. It's a straightforward recipe that brings a staple of Chinese takeout into your kitchen, offering a delicious and satisfying meal that's quicker and healthier than ordering out. The key to achieving tender beef is to slice it thinly against the grain and not overcook it when searing. This dish is perfect for a weeknight dinner and can be easily customized with additional vegetables or adjusted for spiciness to suit your taste.

Chicken Parmesan in a Skillet

Ingredients:

- 4 boneless, skinless chicken breasts, pounded to even thickness
- Salt and freshly ground black pepper, to taste
- 1/2 cup all-purpose flour
- 2 large eggs, beaten
- 1 cup breadcrumbs
- 1/2 cup grated Parmesan cheese
- 2 tablespoons olive oil
- 1 cup marinara sauce
- 1 cup shredded mozzarella cheese
- Fresh basil leaves, for garnish
- Additional grated Parmesan, for serving

Instructions:

1. **Prepare Chicken:** Season both sides of the chicken breasts with salt and pepper. Dredge each chicken breast first in flour, shaking off the excess, then dip in beaten eggs, and finally coat with a mixture of breadcrumbs and grated Parmesan cheese.
2. **Cook Chicken:** Heat olive oil in a large skillet over medium-high heat. Add the chicken breasts and cook until golden brown on each side and cooked through, about 4-5 minutes per side. Remove chicken from the skillet and set aside.
3. **Add Marinara Sauce:** Reduce heat to medium. Pour marinara sauce into the skillet, scraping up any browned bits from the bottom of the pan. Allow the sauce to simmer for a minute to heat through.
4. **Combine Chicken and Sauce:** Return the chicken to the skillet, nestling it into the sauce. Spoon some of the sauce over the top of the chicken.
5. **Add Cheese:** Sprinkle shredded mozzarella cheese over each chicken breast. Cover the skillet with a lid or aluminum foil and cook until the cheese is melted and bubbly, about 3-4 minutes.
6. **Garnish and Serve:** Garnish with fresh basil leaves and additional grated Parmesan. Serve hot directly from the skillet.

Chef's Note:

Chicken Parmesan in a Skillet is a classic Italian-American dish that's been simplified for an easy weeknight meal without sacrificing flavor. This skillet version minimizes cleanup and keeps everything contained for a straightforward cooking process. The key to a perfectly golden and crispy coating is to ensure the chicken is well-coated in the breadcrumb mixture and cooked in hot oil. Using marinara sauce and plenty of cheese turns this into a comforting dish that's sure to please. Serve alongside pasta, garlic bread, or a fresh salad for a complete meal that brings a taste of Italy to your table with minimal fuss.

Bacon-Wrapped Dates with Goat Cheese

Ingredients:

- 24 pitted dates
- 4 ounces goat cheese
- 12 slices of bacon, cut in half
- Toothpicks for securing

Instructions:

1. Preheat Oven: Preheat your oven to 375°F (190°C). Line a baking sheet with parchment paper or a silicone mat for easy cleanup.
2. Stuff Dates: Carefully slice each date along one side to open them up. Stuff each date with a small amount of goat cheese, being careful not to overfill.
3. Wrap Dates: Wrap each stuffed date with a half slice of bacon, securing the ends with a toothpick. Ensure the bacon is snug around the date but not too tight as it will shrink while cooking.
4. Bake: Arrange the bacon-wrapped dates on the prepared baking sheet. Bake in the preheated oven for 20-25 minutes, or until the bacon is crispy and golden brown. Halfway through the baking time, flip each date to ensure even cooking.
5. Serve: Allow the dates to cool slightly on a paper towel-lined plate to absorb any excess grease. Serve warm as a delicious appetizer.

Chef's Note:

Bacon-Wrapped Dates with Goat Cheese are a perfect combination of sweet, salty, and savory flavors, making them an irresistible appetizer for any gathering. The creaminess of the goat cheese complements the natural sweetness of the dates, while the bacon adds a crispy, savory exterior that's hard to beat. This simple yet elegant dish is easy to prepare and can be made ahead of time, then baked just before serving to ensure they are perfectly warm and crispy. For a variation, try adding a toasted almond or pecan inside the date with the goat cheese for an added crunch. Enjoy the delightful contrast of textures and flavors that make this appetizer a crowd-pleaser.

Greek Lemon Chicken Skewers

Ingredients:

- 2 pounds chicken breast, cut into 1-inch cubes
- 1/4 cup olive oil
- Juice and zest of 2 lemons
- 4 cloves garlic, minced
- 2 teaspoons dried oregano
- 1 teaspoon dried thyme
- 1 teaspoon paprika
- Salt and freshly ground black pepper, to taste
- Wooden or metal skewers (if using wooden skewers, soak them in water for at least 30 minutes before grilling)
- Fresh parsley and lemon slices for garnish

Instructions:

1. **Marinate Chicken:** In a large bowl, whisk together olive oil, lemon juice and zest, minced garlic, oregano, thyme, paprika, salt, and pepper. Add the chicken cubes to the marinade, making sure they are well coated. Cover and refrigerate for at least 1 hour, or overnight for best results.
2. **Preheat Grill:** Preheat your grill to medium-high heat.
3. **Prepare Skewers:** Thread the marinated chicken cubes onto the skewers, leaving a small space between each piece for even cooking.
4. **Grill:** Place the skewers on the grill. Cook for 10-12 minutes, turning occasionally, until the chicken is golden brown on all sides and cooked through.
5. **Serve:** Remove the skewers from the grill and let them rest for a few minutes. Garnish with fresh parsley and lemon slices before serving.

Chef's Note:

Greek Lemon Chicken Skewers are a flavorful and healthy option perfect for summer barbecues or any time you're craving a taste of the Mediterranean. The lemon and herbs create a bright and aromatic marinade that infuses the chicken with delicious flavors. Grilling the skewers not only cooks the chicken but also adds a wonderful char that enhances the overall taste. This dish can be served with a variety of sides, such as Greek salad, tzatziki sauce, or warm pita bread, making it a versatile and satisfying meal. Enjoy the combination of simple ingredients coming together to deliver a delightful dining experience.

Sesame Ginger Salmon

Ingredients:

- 4 salmon fillets (about 6 ounces each)
- Salt and freshly ground black pepper, to taste
- 2 tablespoons sesame oil
- 2 tablespoons soy sauce
- 2 tablespoons rice vinegar
- 2 tablespoons honey
- 1 tablespoon fresh ginger, grated
- 2 cloves garlic, minced
- 1 teaspoon sesame seeds, plus more for garnish
- 2 green onions, thinly sliced for garnish

Instructions:

1. Preheat Oven: Preheat your oven to 400°F (200°C).
2. Season Salmon: Lightly season the salmon fillets with salt and pepper.
3. Make the Marinade: In a small bowl, whisk together sesame oil, soy sauce, rice vinegar, honey, grated ginger, and minced garlic.
4. Marinate: Place the salmon fillets in a baking dish. Pour the marinade over the salmon, ensuring each fillet is coated. Let marinate for at least 15 minutes in the refrigerator.
5. Bake: Remove the salmon from the refrigerator. Sprinkle the fillets with sesame seeds. Bake in the preheated oven for 12-15 minutes, or until the salmon flakes easily with a fork.
6. Garnish and Serve: Garnish the baked salmon with additional sesame seeds and sliced green onions. Serve immediately.

Chef's Note:

Sesame Ginger Salmon is a flavorful and healthy dish that combines the rich taste of salmon with the aromatic and zesty flavors of sesame, ginger, and garlic. The marinade not only infuses the salmon with depth of flavor but also creates a delicious glaze as it bakes. This dish is simple to prepare, making it perfect for a quick weeknight dinner or a special occasion. The combination of ingredients ensures that each bite is moist, flavorful, and packed with nutrients. Serve this salmon with a side of steamed vegetables or rice for a complete meal that's sure to impress. Enjoy the perfect balance of sweet, savory, and umami flavors in this elegant and satisfying dish.

Easy Chicken Piccata

Ingredients:

- 4 boneless, skinless chicken breasts, pounded to even thickness
- Salt and freshly ground black pepper, to taste
- 1/2 cup all-purpose flour, for dredging
- 2 tablespoons olive oil
- 2 tablespoons unsalted butter, divided
- 1/4 cup fresh lemon juice
- 1/2 cup chicken broth
- 1/4 cup capers, rinsed
- 2 tablespoons fresh parsley, chopped

Instructions:

1. Prepare Chicken: Season both sides of the chicken breasts with salt and pepper. Dredge the chicken in flour, shaking off the excess.
2. Cook Chicken: Heat the olive oil and 1 tablespoon of butter in a large skillet over medium-high heat. Add the chicken and cook until golden brown on both sides and cooked through, about 3-4 minutes per side. Remove chicken from the skillet and set aside.
3. Make the Sauce: In the same skillet, add lemon juice, chicken broth, and capers. Bring to a simmer, scraping up any browned bits from the bottom of the skillet. Reduce the sauce for about 2 minutes to thicken slightly.
4. Finish the Dish: Return the chicken to the skillet and simmer in the sauce for 1 minute. Remove from heat and stir in the remaining tablespoon of butter until melted and the sauce is glossy.
5. Serve: Transfer the chicken to plates, spoon the caper-lemon sauce over the top, and garnish with chopped parsley.

Chef's Note:

Easy Chicken Piccata is a classic Italian dish that's light, flavorful, and quick to prepare, making it perfect for a weeknight dinner. The combination of lemon, capers, and parsley offers a bright and tangy flavor that beautifully complements the tender chicken. This dish is traditionally served with pasta, rice, or steamed vegetables to soak up the delicious sauce. Chicken Piccata is a wonderful example of how simple ingredients can create a meal that's both elegant and satisfying. Enjoy the fresh and zesty flavors of this beloved Italian classic in the comfort of your own home.

Pan-Seared Duck Breast with Orange Sauce

Ingredients:
- 2 duck breasts, skin on
- Salt and freshly ground black pepper, to taste
- 1 tablespoon olive oil
- 1/2 cup fresh orange juice
- 1/4 cup chicken broth
- 2 tablespoons honey
- 1 tablespoon soy sauce
- 1 teaspoon orange zest
- 2 cloves garlic, minced
- 1 teaspoon fresh thyme leaves
- 2 tablespoons unsalted butter

Instructions:

1. **Prepare Duck Breasts:** Score the skin of the duck breasts in a crosshatch pattern, being careful not to cut into the flesh. Season both sides with salt and pepper.
2. **Cook Duck Breasts:** Heat olive oil in a skillet over medium heat. Place the duck breasts skin-side down and cook until the skin is golden and crispy, about 5-7 minutes. Flip and cook on the flesh side for another 4-5 minutes for medium-rare. Remove from the skillet and let rest.
3. **Make Orange Sauce:** In the same skillet, discard excess fat but keep the flavorful bits. Add orange juice, chicken broth, honey, soy sauce, orange zest, minced garlic, and thyme. Bring to a simmer and reduce by half, about 5-8 minutes. Whisk in the butter until the sauce is glossy.
4. **Serve:** Slice the duck breasts thinly. Drizzle with the orange sauce and serve immediately.

Chef's Note:

Pan-Seared Duck Breast with Orange Sauce is a luxurious dish that combines the rich flavor of duck with a vibrant, citrusy sauce. The key to perfectly cooked duck is rendering the fat from the skin to achieve a crispy exterior while keeping the inside juicy and tender. The orange sauce, with its sweet and tangy flavors, complements the duck beautifully, creating a balanced and sophisticated meal. This dish is sure to impress at any dinner party or special occasion, offering an elegant dining experience that's surprisingly simple to prepare at home. Serve with a side of roasted vegetables or a fresh salad for a complete gourmet meal.

Fish and Seafood

Dive into the bountiful seas and discover a treasure trove of flavors with our collection of fish and seafood recipes. Imagine the salty breeze and the ocean's freshness as you savor the perfect sear on a scallop or the tender, flaky texture of a beautifully cooked salmon fillet.

Each recipe is a journey through the vast culinary depths of the ocean, crafted to simplify the art of preparing seafood while keeping the taste, delight, and accessibility at the forefront. From the zesty excitement of lemon-garlic shrimp skewers to the comforting embrace of a hearty fish stew, we invite you to explore the wide array of healthful and mouthwatering dishes that the sea has to offer. Embrace the beneficial omega-3s, the lean proteins, and the rich tapestry of flavors that fish and seafood provide.

This collection is your guide to transforming everyday meals into extraordinary culinary experiences, celebrating the diversity and the beauty of the ocean's bounty.

Lemon Butter Baked Cod Delight

Ingredients:

- 4 cod fillets (about 6 ounces each)
- Salt and freshly ground black pepper, to taste
- 4 tablespoons unsalted butter, melted
- Juice of 1 lemon
- 2 teaspoons lemon zest
- 2 cloves garlic, minced
- 1 tablespoon fresh parsley, chopped
- 1 teaspoon dried thyme
- Lemon slices, for garnish

Instructions:

1. Preheat Oven: Preheat your oven to 400°F (200°C). Lightly grease a baking dish.
2. Season Cod: Season both sides of the cod fillets with salt and pepper. Place them in the prepared baking dish.
3. Prepare Lemon Butter Mixture: In a small bowl, combine melted butter, lemon juice, lemon zest, minced garlic, parsley, and thyme. Stir well to mix.
4. Bake: Pour the lemon butter mixture over the cod fillets, ensuring they are well coated. Top each fillet with a lemon slice. Bake in the preheated oven for 12-15 minutes, or until the fish flakes easily with a fork.
5. Serve: Remove from the oven and spoon any of the pan sauces over the cod before serving. Garnish with additional fresh parsley if desired.

Chef's Note:

Lemon Butter Baked Cod Delight is a light, flavorful dish that brings the essence of the sea to your dining table. The combination of lemon and butter creates a succulent sauce that perfectly complements the delicate taste of cod, while garlic, parsley, and thyme add depth and aroma to each bite. This dish is an excellent choice for a healthy, satisfying meal that's easy to prepare, making it perfect for busy weeknights or a special occasion. Serve with a side of roasted vegetables or a fresh salad for a complete, nutritious meal. Enjoy the delightful interplay of flavors and the simplicity of this elegant seafood creation.

Garlic Shrimp Zoodle Toss

Ingredients:

- 1 pound large shrimp, peeled and deveined
- Salt and freshly ground black pepper, to taste
- 3 tablespoons olive oil, divided
- 4 cloves garlic, minced
- 1/2 teaspoon red pepper flakes (optional for heat)
- 4 medium zucchinis, spiralized into noodles (zoodles)
- Juice of 1 lemon
- 1/4 cup grated Parmesan cheese
- 2 tablespoons fresh parsley, chopped
- Lemon wedges, for serving

Instructions:

1. Season Shrimp: Season the shrimp with salt and pepper.
2. Cook Shrimp: In a large skillet over medium-high heat, heat 2 tablespoons of olive oil. Add the shrimp and cook until they are pink and opaque, about 2 minutes per side. Add the garlic and red pepper flakes (if using) during the last minute of cooking. Transfer the shrimp to a plate and set aside.
3. Cook Zoodles: In the same skillet, add the remaining tablespoon of olive oil. Add the zoodles and sauté for about 2-3 minutes until just tender. Be careful not to overcook.
4. Combine: Return the shrimp to the skillet with the zoodles. Add the lemon juice and toss to combine. Heat through for about 1 minute.
5. Serve: Sprinkle with grated Parmesan cheese and fresh parsley. Serve immediately with lemon wedges on the side.

Chef's Note:

Garlic Shrimp Zoodle Toss is a light, flavorful, and healthy alternative to traditional pasta dishes. The zoodles offer a fresh and nutritious base, perfectly complementing the succulent shrimp seasoned with garlic and a hint of heat from the red pepper flakes. This dish is not only easy to make but also quick, making it an ideal choice for a busy weeknight dinner that doesn't compromise on taste or health. The lemon juice adds a bright zestiness, while the Parmesan cheese brings a savory depth. Enjoy this delightful blend of flavors and textures for a satisfying meal that's both comforting and guilt-free.

Crispy Coconut Crusted Tilapia

Ingredients:

- 4 tilapia fillets
- Salt and freshly ground black pepper, to taste
- 1/2 cup all-purpose flour
- 2 large eggs, beaten
- 1 cup shredded coconut
- 1/2 cup panko breadcrumbs
- 2 tablespoons olive oil or coconut oil, for frying
- Lime wedges, for serving
- Fresh cilantro, for garnish

Instructions:

1. Prepare the Fillets: Season the tilapia fillets with salt and pepper on both sides.
2. Dredge the Fillets: Place the flour, beaten eggs, and a mixture of shredded coconut and panko breadcrumbs in three separate shallow dishes. Dredge each fillet in flour, shaking off the excess, then dip in the beaten eggs, and finally coat evenly with the coconut-panko mixture.
3. Fry the Tilapia: Heat the oil in a large skillet over medium heat. Fry the coated fillets until golden brown and crispy, about 3-4 minutes per side, depending on the thickness. Transfer to a paper towel-lined plate to drain any excess oil.
4. Serve: Serve the crispy tilapia with lime wedges and garnish with fresh cilantro.

Chef's Note:

Crispy Coconut Crusted Tilapia is a delightful twist on traditional fried fish, offering a tropical flair with its crunchy coconut-panko crust. This dish is not only visually appealing but also packed with flavor, with the coconut adding a sweet contrast to the mild, tender tilapia. It's a simple yet impressive recipe that's perfect for a quick weeknight dinner or a special occasion. Frying in coconut oil can enhance the coconut flavor, but olive oil works well for a lighter taste. Serve with a side of rice, a fresh salad, or steamed vegetables to complete this delicious meal. Enjoy the crispy exterior and juicy interior of this beautifully prepared fish, enhanced by the zestiness of lime and the freshness of cilantro.

Honey Glazed Salmon with Ginger

Ingredients:

- 4 salmon fillets (about 6 ounces each)
- Salt and freshly ground black pepper, to taste
- 1/4 cup honey
- 2 tablespoons soy sauce
- 1 tablespoon fresh ginger, grated
- 2 cloves garlic, minced
- 1 tablespoon olive oil
- 1 tablespoon fresh lemon juice
- 1 teaspoon sesame seeds, for garnish
- Fresh green onions, thinly sliced, for garnish

Instructions:

1. Prepare the Salmon: Season the salmon fillets with salt and pepper on both sides.
2. Make the Glaze: In a small bowl, whisk together the honey, soy sauce, grated ginger, minced garlic, and lemon juice until well combined.
3. Cook the Salmon: Heat the olive oil in a large skillet over medium-high heat. Add the salmon fillets, skin-side down, and cook for about 4 minutes until the skin is crispy. Flip the fillets over and cook for another 2 minutes.
4. Glaze the Salmon: Reduce the heat to low. Pour the honey ginger glaze over the salmon fillets in the skillet. Cook for another 2-3 minutes, spooning the glaze over the fillets as they cook.
5. Garnish and Serve: Transfer the glazed salmon to plates. Sprinkle with sesame seeds and garnish with sliced green onions. Serve immediately.

Chef's Note:

Honey Glazed Salmon with Ginger is a delightful dish that combines the natural richness of salmon with the sweet and tangy flavors of honey and ginger. The glaze creates a beautifully caramelized surface on the salmon, adding depth and complexity to each bite. This recipe is not only delicious but also quick and easy to prepare, making it perfect for a healthy weeknight dinner or a special occasion. The addition of fresh lemon juice brightens the dish, while the sesame seeds and green onions provide a textural contrast and a burst of color. Enjoy this elegant and flavorful meal that's sure to impress both family and guests.

Simple Spicy Tuna Poke Bowl

Ingredients:

- 1 pound sushi-grade tuna, diced
- 1/4 cup soy sauce
- 1 tablespoon sesame oil
- 1 tablespoon rice vinegar
- 1 teaspoon honey
- 1-2 teaspoons sriracha sauce, adjust to taste
- 1 teaspoon fresh ginger, grated
- 2 cups cooked sushi rice or brown rice, cooled
- 1 avocado, diced
- 1/2 cucumber, thinly sliced
- 1/4 cup scallions, chopped
- 1 tablespoon sesame seeds
- Optional garnishes: seaweed salad, pickled ginger, wasabi

Instructions:

1. Prepare Tuna Mixture: In a medium bowl, mix together diced tuna, soy sauce, sesame oil, rice vinegar, honey, sriracha sauce, and grated ginger. Stir well to combine. Refrigerate for at least 15 minutes to marinate.
2. Assemble Poke Bowls: Divide the cooked rice between bowls. Top with marinated tuna, diced avocado, sliced cucumber, and chopped scallions.
3. Garnish: Sprinkle sesame seeds over the top. Add optional garnishes like seaweed salad, pickled ginger, and wasabi to taste.
4. Serve: Enjoy your Simple Spicy Tuna Poke Bowl immediately, offering a refreshing and satisfying meal.

Chef's Note:

This Simple Spicy Tuna Poke Bowl brings a piece of Hawaiian cuisine right to your table with minimal effort. It's a harmonious blend of flavors and textures, from the tender, marinated tuna to the creamy avocado and crisp cucumber. The spicy marinade adds a delightful kick that can be adjusted to suit your preference. Poke bowls are incredibly versatile, so feel free to customize with your favorite toppings and sides for a personalized dining experience. This dish is not only a feast for the eyes but also packed with healthy ingredients, making it a perfect option for a nutritious and delicious meal any day of the week.

Mediterranean Sea Bass en Papillote

Ingredients:

- 4 sea bass fillets (about 6 ounces each)
- Salt and freshly ground black pepper, to taste
- 2 tablespoons olive oil
- 1 lemon, thinly sliced
- 2 tomatoes, thinly sliced
- 1 small red onion, thinly sliced
- 2 cloves garlic, minced
- 1/4 cup kalamata olives, pitted and halved
- 2 tablespoons capers, drained
- 1 teaspoon dried oregano
- 1 teaspoon dried thyme
- Fresh parsley, chopped, for garnish

Instructions:

1. Preheat Oven: Preheat your oven to 400°F (200°C).
2. Prepare Parchment Paper: Cut four large squares of parchment paper, big enough to wrap each fish fillet completely.
3. Season Fish: Season both sides of the sea bass fillets with salt and pepper. Place a fillet in the center of each piece of parchment paper.
4. Add Toppings: Drizzle olive oil over each fillet. Top with lemon slices, tomato slices, red onion slices, minced garlic, kalamata olives, and capers. Sprinkle with oregano and thyme.
5. Wrap Fillets: Fold the parchment paper over the fish, twisting the ends to seal and create a packet (en papillote).
6. Bake: Place the packets on a baking sheet. Bake for 15-20 minutes, or until the fish is cooked through and the packets have puffed up.
7. Serve: Carefully open the packets (watch for steam), and transfer the contents to plates. Garnish with fresh parsley before serving.

Chef's Note:

Mediterranean Sea Bass en Papillote is a simple yet elegant dish that steams the fish in its own juices, locking in flavor and moisture. This cooking method, combined with the bright flavors of lemon, tomato, olives, and herbs, creates a deliciously light and healthy meal that's perfect for any occasion. Cooking en papillote is not only a visually impressive way to serve fish but also a healthy cooking technique that preserves nutrients. This recipe can be easily adapted to include other vegetables or herbs based on preference. Enjoy the delightful medley of Mediterranean flavors in this hassle-free and delicious dish.

Parmesan-Herb Crusted Haddock

Ingredients:

- 4 haddock fillets (about 6 ounces each)
- Salt and freshly ground black pepper, to taste
- 1/2 cup grated Parmesan cheese
- 1/4 cup breadcrumbs
- 2 tablespoons fresh parsley, finely chopped
- 1 tablespoon fresh thyme leaves, finely chopped
- 2 cloves garlic, minced
- 2 tablespoons olive oil
- Lemon wedges, for serving

Instructions:

1. Preheat Oven: Preheat your oven to 400°F (200°C). Line a baking sheet with parchment paper.
2. Season Fillets: Season both sides of the haddock fillets with salt and pepper.
3. Prepare Parmesan-Herb Mixture: In a bowl, combine grated Parmesan, breadcrumbs, parsley, thyme, and minced garlic. Mix well.
4. Coat Fillets: Brush each fillet with olive oil, then press the Parmesan-herb mixture onto the top side of each fillet, ensuring a good coat.
5. Bake: Place the coated fillets on the prepared baking sheet. Bake in the preheated oven for 12-15 minutes, or until the fish flakes easily with a fork and the crust is golden and crispy.
6. Serve: Serve the haddock fillets immediately with lemon wedges on the side.

Chef's Note:

Parmesan-Herb Crusted Haddock is a deliciously elegant dish that combines the delicate flavors of haddock with a crispy, flavorful crust. The Parmesan cheese provides a savory depth, while the herbs add freshness and the breadcrumbs create the perfect crunchy texture. This recipe is simple to prepare, making it an excellent choice for a quick weeknight dinner that feels special enough for entertaining. The lemon wedges add a bright burst of flavor, enhancing the overall dish. Enjoy this healthy, flavorful meal that's sure to impress with its balance of textures and tastes.

Savory Shrimp and Grits Comfort

Ingredients:

- **For the Grits:**
- 1 cup stone-ground grits
- 4 cups water
- 1 teaspoon salt
- 1/2 cup heavy cream
- 1/4 cup grated Parmesan cheese
- 2 tablespoons unsalted butter

- **For the Shrimp:**
- 1 pound large shrimp, peeled and deveined
- Salt and freshly ground black pepper, to taste
- 2 tablespoons olive oil
- 1 small onion, finely chopped
- 1 bell pepper, finely chopped
- 2 cloves garlic, minced
- 1/2 teaspoon smoked paprika
- 1/4 teaspoon cayenne pepper
- 1/2 cup chicken broth
- 2 tablespoons fresh lemon juice
- 2 tablespoons fresh parsley, chopped

Instructions:

1. Cook Grits: In a medium saucepan, bring water and salt to a boil. Whisk in grits and reduce heat to low. Cover and simmer, stirring occasionally, until grits are thick and creamy, about 20-25 minutes. Stir in heavy cream, Parmesan cheese, and butter until well combined. Adjust seasoning with salt and pepper. Keep warm.
2. Prepare Shrimp: Season shrimp with salt, black pepper, smoked paprika, and cayenne pepper.
3. Cook Shrimp: Heat olive oil in a large skillet over medium heat. Add onion and bell pepper, sautéing until soft, about 5 minutes. Add garlic and cook for another minute until fragrant.
4. Add Shrimp to Skillet: Add seasoned shrimp to the skillet and cook until pink and opaque, about 2-3 minutes per side. Pour in chicken broth and lemon juice, simmering for 2 minutes to let flavors meld.
5. Serve: Spoon creamy grits onto plates. Top with shrimp mixture and garnish with chopped parsley.

Chef's Note:

Savory Shrimp and Grits Comfort is a classic Southern dish that embodies the essence of home cooking. This recipe combines creamy, buttery grits with spicy, succulent shrimp for a meal that's both comforting and sophisticated. The combination of smoked paprika and cayenne pepper adds a delightful warmth that complements the richness of the grits, making each bite a harmonious blend of flavors and textures. Whether it's for a cozy family dinner or a casual gathering, this dish is sure to impress with its depth of flavor and satisfying heartiness. Enjoy this Southern comfort classic that brings warmth and happiness to any table.

Clam and Chorizo Paella Fiesta

Ingredients:

- 2 tablespoons olive oil
- 1/2 pound chorizo, sliced
- 1 onion, finely chopped
- 3 cloves garlic, minced
- 1 red bell pepper, diced
- 1 cup short-grain paella rice (e.g., Bomba or Arborio)
- 1/2 teaspoon saffron threads, crushed
- 1 teaspoon smoked paprika
- 2 cups chicken broth
- 1 cup diced tomatoes (canned or fresh)
- 1 pound clams, scrubbed
- 1/2 cup frozen peas, thawed
- Salt and freshly ground black pepper, to taste
- Lemon wedges, for serving
- Fresh parsley, chopped, for garnish

Instructions:

1. **Cook Chorizo:** Heat olive oil in a large paella pan or wide skillet over medium heat. Add chorizo and cook until browned and crispy. Remove chorizo and set aside.
2. **Sauté Vegetables:** In the same pan, add onion, garlic, and bell pepper. Cook until the vegetables are soft and fragrant.
3. **Add Rice and Spices:** Stir in the rice, saffron, and smoked paprika, coating the rice with the oil and spices. Cook for 2 minutes.
4. **Add Liquids:** Pour in chicken broth and diced tomatoes. Season with salt and pepper. Bring to a simmer, then reduce heat to low. Cook, without stirring, until rice is almost tender, about 15-20 minutes.
5. **Add Seafood:** Nestle the clams into the rice. Cover the pan and cook until the clams have opened and the rice is tender, about 5-10 minutes. Discard any unopened clams.
6. **Final Touches:** Stir in the cooked chorizo and peas. Cook for an additional 2 minutes to heat through.
7. **Serve:** Garnish with fresh parsley and serve with lemon wedges on the side.

Chef's Note:

Clam and Chorizo Paella Fiesta is a vibrant, flavor-packed dish that brings the essence of Spanish cuisine to your table. The combination of the spicy chorizo with the fresh clams creates a delightful contrast, while the saffron and smoked paprika provide a depth of flavor and color to the dish. This recipe is perfect for entertaining, offering a festive and communal meal that's as fun to cook as it is to eat. Paella is all about technique and timing, so make sure to have all your ingredients prepped and ready to go for a smooth cooking experience. Enjoy this fiesta of flavors with family and friends for a memorable meal.

Sweet and Sour Grilled Mackerel

Ingredients:

- 4 mackerel fillets
- Salt and freshly ground black pepper, to taste
- 2 tablespoons olive oil

- **For the Sweet and Sour Sauce:**
- 1/4 cup rice vinegar
- 1/4 cup brown sugar
- 2 tablespoons soy sauce
- 1 tablespoon ketchup
- 1 teaspoon cornstarch mixed with 1 tablespoon water
- 1 garlic clove, minced
- 1 teaspoon ginger, grated
- 1/2 teaspoon red pepper flakes (optional)

Instructions:

1. Preheat Grill: Preheat your grill to medium-high heat.
2. Season Mackerel: Brush the mackerel fillets with olive oil and season with salt and pepper on both sides.
3. Grill Mackerel: Place the fillets skin-side down on the grill. Grill for about 4-5 minutes per side, or until the skin is crispy and the flesh flakes easily.
4. Prepare Sweet and Sour Sauce: While the mackerel is grilling, combine rice vinegar, brown sugar, soy sauce, ketchup, garlic, ginger, and red pepper flakes in a small saucepan over medium heat. Stir until the sugar has dissolved. Add the cornstarch mixture and stir continuously until the sauce thickens, about 2-3 minutes.
5. Serve: Drizzle the sweet and sour sauce over the grilled mackerel fillets. Serve immediately.

Chef's Note:

Sweet and Sour Grilled Mackerel is a delightful twist on the traditional grilled fish, introducing a vibrant combination of flavors that perfectly complements the rich, oily nature of mackerel. This dish balances the fish's natural savory taste with the tangy sweetness of the sauce, making each bite a flavorful experience. The crispy skin of the grilled mackerel, paired with the sticky, sweet, and slightly spicy sauce, creates a textural and taste contrast that's truly irresistible. This recipe is simple, quick, and perfect for a nutritious and satisfying meal any day of the week. Enjoy the unique blend of flavors that this dish brings to your table, showcasing the versatility of mackerel in a whole new light.

Vegetarian and Vegan

Here is the Vegetarian and Vegan section, which will take your taste buds on a rollercoaster ride through the plant-based paradise where the greens are the bosses. Here, colors and flavors never fade.

This section of our cookbook seeks to celebrate the bounty of nature, truly meant to inspire even the most dyed-in-the-wool meat eater with the richness of vegetarian and vegan fare. From rainbow salads to hearty legume stews, the sheer intensity and variety of tastes are an ode to what is possible without a single animal. Discover new ways of how to turn the vegetables, fruits, grains, and legumes to become something tasty for your body—something that won't only respond to your cravings but also nourish your body.

Whether you're well practiced in vegan eating or looking to add more plant-based meals to your weekly routine, these recipes will leave you itching to try new things. Join us to bring power to your plate, and enjoy boundless possibilities with vegetarian and vegan dishes.

Creamy Avocado Spinach Pasta

Ingredients:

- 12 ounces pasta (such as spaghetti or fettuccine)
- 2 ripe avocados, pitted and scooped
- 2 cups fresh spinach leaves
- 1/4 cup fresh basil leaves
- 2 cloves garlic
- 2 tablespoons lemon juice
- 1/3 cup olive oil
- Salt and freshly ground black pepper, to taste
- 1/2 cup grated Parmesan cheese (optional for vegan, substitute with nutritional yeast)
- Cherry tomatoes for garnish
- Additional fresh basil, for garnish

Instructions:

1. Cook Pasta: Cook the pasta according to package instructions in a large pot of salted boiling water until al dente. Reserve 1 cup of pasta water, then drain and set aside.
2. Make Avocado Sauce: In a food processor, combine the avocados, spinach, basil, garlic, and lemon juice. Pulse until smooth. With the processor running, slowly add the olive oil until the mixture is creamy. Season with salt and pepper to taste.
3. Combine Pasta and Sauce: Return the cooked pasta to the pot. Over low heat, add the avocado sauce to the pasta, tossing to coat evenly. If the sauce is too thick, add a little reserved pasta water until you reach the desired consistency.
4. Serve: Transfer the creamy pasta to serving dishes. Sprinkle with grated Parmesan cheese or nutritional yeast, garnish with cherry tomatoes and additional basil leaves. Serve immediately.

Chef's Note:

Creamy Avocado Spinach Pasta is a lush, vibrant dish that brings together the richness of avocado with the freshness of spinach and basil for a delightfully green and healthy meal. This dish is incredibly versatile, perfect for a quick lunch or a comforting dinner. The creamy texture of the sauce, achieved without any dairy (unless you opt for Parmesan), makes it a fantastic option for both vegetarians and vegans. The lemon juice not only adds a bright note to the sauce but also helps preserve the vivid green color. Enjoy this easy-to-make, nutritious pasta that's sure to be a hit with everyone at the table.

Quinoa Stuffed Bell Peppers Delight

Ingredients:

- 4 large bell peppers, halved and seeds removed
- 1 cup quinoa, rinsed
- 2 cups vegetable broth
- 1 tablespoon olive oil
- 1 small onion, diced
- 2 cloves garlic, minced
- 1 zucchini, diced
- 1 cup black beans, drained and rinsed
- 1 cup corn kernels (fresh or frozen)
- 1 teaspoon ground cumin
- 1 teaspoon chili powder
- 1/2 teaspoon paprika
- Salt and freshly ground black pepper, to taste
- 1 cup grated cheddar cheese or vegan cheese alternative
- Fresh cilantro, for garnish
- Avocado slices and lime wedges, for serving

Instructions:

1. **Preheat Oven and Prepare Peppers:** Preheat your oven to 375°F (190°C). Arrange the bell pepper halves in a baking dish, cut-side up.
2. **Cook Quinoa:** In a medium saucepan, bring the vegetable broth to a boil. Add the quinoa, reduce heat to low, cover, and simmer for 15-20 minutes, or until the liquid is absorbed and the quinoa is fluffy.
3. **Sauté Vegetables:** While the quinoa cooks, heat the olive oil in a skillet over medium heat. Add the onion and garlic, and sauté until soft. Add the zucchini, black beans, corn, cumin, chili powder, paprika, salt, and pepper. Cook for another 5-7 minutes, until the vegetables are tender.
4. **Combine Quinoa and Vegetable Mixture:** Mix the cooked quinoa into the skillet with the vegetable mixture. Stir well to combine.
5. **Stuff the Peppers:** Spoon the quinoa and vegetable mixture into each bell pepper half. Top with grated cheese.
6. **Bake:** Cover the baking dish with aluminum foil and bake for about 30 minutes. Remove the foil and bake for an additional 10 minutes, or until the cheese is melted and bubbly.
7. **Serve:** Garnish with fresh cilantro and serve with avocado slices and lime wedges on the side.

Chef's Note:

Quinoa Stuffed Bell Peppers Delight is a colorful, nutritious, and satisfying meal that's perfect for any occasion. This recipe is a great way to enjoy a variety of vegetables and protein-rich quinoa, all packed into a delicious and edible container. The spices add a wonderful depth of flavor, while the cheese (or vegan alternative) provides a creamy topping that perfectly complements the filling. This dish is easily customizable, so feel free to add or substitute ingredients based on your preferences. Whether you're serving a family dinner or looking for a show-stopping vegetarian main, these stuffed peppers are sure to impress.

Hearty Lentil and Mushroom Stew

Ingredients:

- 1 cup dried green or brown lentils, rinsed
- 2 tablespoons olive oil
- 1 onion, diced
- 2 carrots, diced
- 2 celery stalks, diced
- 3 cloves garlic, minced
- 8 ounces mushrooms, sliced (any variety)
- 4 cups vegetable broth
- 1 can (14 ounces) diced tomatoes, undrained
- 2 teaspoons dried thyme
- 1 teaspoon dried rosemary
- Salt and freshly ground black pepper, to taste
- 2 bay leaves
- Fresh parsley, chopped, for garnish

Instructions:

1. Sauté Vegetables: In a large pot, heat olive oil over medium heat. Add onion, carrots, and celery. Sauté until the vegetables start to soften, about 5 minutes. Add garlic and mushrooms, and continue to cook until mushrooms are browned, about 5 more minutes.
2. Add Lentils and Liquids: Stir in the lentils, vegetable broth, diced tomatoes with their juice, thyme, rosemary, salt, pepper, and bay leaves. Bring to a boil, then reduce heat to low. Cover and simmer for 25-30 minutes, or until lentils are tender.
3. Finish the Stew: Remove the bay leaves. If desired, use an immersion blender to partially blend the stew for a thicker consistency, leaving some lentils and vegetables whole for texture.
4. Serve: Ladle the stew into bowls and garnish with fresh parsley. Serve hot.

Chef's Note:

This Hearty Lentil and Mushroom Stew is a comforting and nourishing meal, perfect for chilly evenings or any time you crave a warm, satisfying dish. Lentils and mushrooms provide a fantastic combination of flavors and textures, while the aromatic herbs add depth to the rich, savory broth. This stew is not only delicious but also packed with nutrients, making it a great choice for those seeking a healthy, plant-based option. It's versatile enough to be enjoyed on its own or served alongside crusty bread for dipping. Dive into this bowl of coziness, and let it warm your heart and stomach.

Chickpea Curry in a Hurry

Ingredients:

- 2 tablespoons olive oil
- 1 large onion, finely chopped
- 2 cloves garlic, minced
- 1 tablespoon fresh ginger, grated
- 1 tablespoon curry powder
- 1 teaspoon ground turmeric
- 1/2 teaspoon cayenne pepper (optional, adjust to taste)
- 1 can (14 ounces) diced tomatoes
- 2 cans (14 ounces each) chickpeas, drained and rinsed
- 1 can (14 ounces) coconut milk
- Salt and freshly ground black pepper, to taste
- Fresh cilantro, chopped, for garnish
- Cooked rice, for serving

Instructions:

1. Sauté Aromatics: In a large skillet or saucepan, heat the olive oil over medium heat. Add the onion, garlic, and ginger, cooking until the onion is translucent and soft, about 5 minutes.
2. Add Spices: Stir in the curry powder, turmeric, and cayenne pepper, cooking for another minute until the spices are fragrant.
3. Combine Ingredients: Add the diced tomatoes (with their juice), chickpeas, and coconut milk to the skillet. Season with salt and pepper to taste. Stir well to combine all the ingredients.
4. Simmer: Bring the mixture to a simmer, then reduce the heat to low. Cover and let it cook for 15-20 minutes, allowing the flavors to meld together.
5. Serve: Ladle the curry over cooked rice and garnish with chopped cilantro. Serve hot.

Chef's Note:

Chickpea Curry in a Hurry is your go-to recipe for when you need a flavorful, nourishing meal without spending hours in the kitchen. This dish combines the hearty textures of chickpeas with the rich, aromatic flavors of curry and coconut milk, creating a comforting and satisfying meal. It's perfect for busy weeknights, easily adaptable to your heat preference, and packed with plant-based protein. Serve it over a bed of rice for a complete meal that's both filling and delightful. Embrace the simplicity and taste of this quick curry that's sure to become a staple in your culinary repertoire.

Vegan Tofu Scramble Fiesta

Ingredients:

- 1 block (14 ounces) firm tofu, drained and pressed
- 2 tablespoons olive oil
- 1/2 onion, diced
- 1 bell pepper, diced (any color)
- 1/2 cup black beans, drained and rinsed
- 1/2 cup corn kernels (fresh or frozen)
- 1 tomato, diced
- 1 teaspoon turmeric powder
- 1/2 teaspoon paprika
- 1/2 teaspoon ground cumin
- Salt and freshly ground black pepper, to taste
- 1/4 cup nutritional yeast (optional for cheesy flavor)
- Fresh cilantro, chopped, for garnish
- Avocado slices, for serving
- Salsa and lime wedges, for serving

Instructions:

1. Crumble the Tofu: Using your hands or a fork, crumble the pressed tofu into bite-sized pieces.
2. Cook the Vegetables: Heat the olive oil in a large skillet over medium heat. Add the onion and bell pepper, sautéing until softened, about 5 minutes. Stir in the black beans, corn, and tomato, cooking for an additional 3 minutes.
3. Add Tofu and Spices: Add the crumbled tofu to the skillet along with the turmeric, paprika, cumin, salt, and pepper. Cook, stirring frequently, for about 8-10 minutes, until the tofu is heated through and starts to get a slight golden color.
4. Finish with Nutritional Yeast: If using, sprinkle nutritional yeast over the scramble and stir well to combine, cooking for another 2 minutes.
5. Serve: Garnish with fresh cilantro and serve the tofu scramble with avocado slices on the side. Offer salsa and lime wedges for extra flavor.

Chef's Note:

Vegan Tofu Scramble Fiesta is a vibrant, hearty dish that brings a plant-based twist to the traditional breakfast scramble. Packed with vegetables and spices, this recipe not only delivers on flavor but also on nutrition, making it a fantastic start to the day or a satisfying meal any time. The turmeric gives the tofu its characteristic yellow hue, mimicking the look of scrambled eggs, while the spices infuse it with a depth of flavor. Nutritional yeast adds a cheesy, nutty taste and boosts the nutritional profile. Enjoy this colorful, flavorful fiesta in a bowl, perfect for anyone looking to add more plant-based options to their meal rotation.

Roasted Butternut Squash Soup

Ingredients:

- 1 large butternut squash (about 2 pounds), peeled, seeded, and cubed
- 3 tablespoons olive oil, divided
- Salt and freshly ground black pepper, to taste
- 1 medium onion, chopped
- 2 cloves garlic, minced
- 4 cups vegetable broth
- 1 teaspoon fresh thyme leaves
- 1/2 teaspoon ground cinnamon
- 1/4 teaspoon ground nutmeg
- 1 cup coconut milk
- Pumpkin seeds, for garnish
- Fresh thyme, for garnish

Instructions:

1. Roast the Squash: Preheat your oven to 400°F (200°C). Toss the butternut squash cubes with 2 tablespoons of olive oil, salt, and pepper. Spread them out on a baking sheet and roast for 25-30 minutes, or until tender and lightly caramelized.
2. Sauté Onion and Garlic: While the squash is roasting, heat the remaining tablespoon of olive oil in a large pot over medium heat. Add the onion and garlic, sautéing until soft and translucent, about 5 minutes.
3. Simmer Soup: Add the roasted butternut squash to the pot along with the vegetable broth, thyme leaves, cinnamon, and nutmeg. Bring to a simmer and let cook for 15 minutes, allowing the flavors to meld together.
4. Blend the Soup: Using an immersion blender, purée the soup directly in the pot until smooth. Alternatively, you can use a regular blender, working in batches if necessary.
5. Finish with Coconut Milk: Stir in the coconut milk and heat through. Adjust seasoning with salt and pepper as needed.
6. Serve: Ladle the soup into bowls and garnish with pumpkin seeds and a sprig of fresh thyme.

Chef's Note:

Roasted Butternut Squash Soup is a warm, comforting dish perfect for chilly days. Roasting the squash enhances its natural sweetness and adds depth to the soup's flavor. The addition of coconut milk gives this soup a creamy texture without the need for dairy, making it a great vegan option. The spices, thyme, cinnamon, and nutmeg, offer a subtle warmth and complexity. This soup is not only delicious but also packed with vitamins and nutrients. It can be served as a starter for a festive meal or enjoyed as a main course with crusty bread for a cozy, satisfying dinner.

Zesty Black Bean and Corn Tacos

Ingredients:

- 1 can (15 ounces) black beans, drained and rinsed
- 1 cup corn kernels (fresh, frozen, or canned)
- 1 avocado, diced
- 1/2 red onion, finely chopped
- 1/4 cup fresh cilantro, chopped
- Juice of 2 limes
- 1 teaspoon chili powder
- Salt and freshly ground black pepper, to taste
- 8 small corn tortillas
- 1/2 cup crumbled feta cheese or vegan cheese alternative
- Optional garnishes: sliced jalapeños, sour cream or vegan yogurt, lime wedges

Instructions:

1. Prepare Filling: In a large bowl, combine black beans, corn, avocado, red onion, cilantro, lime juice, chili powder, salt, and pepper. Mix well to combine.
2. Warm Tortillas: Heat the tortillas in a dry skillet over medium heat for about 30 seconds on each side, or until warm and slightly charred.
3. Assemble Tacos: Spoon the black bean and corn mixture onto each tortilla. Top with crumbled feta cheese or vegan cheese alternative.
4. Serve: Garnish with optional sliced jalapeños, a dollop of sour cream or vegan yogurt, and lime wedges on the side.

Chef's Note:

Zesty Black Bean and Corn Tacos are a vibrant, flavorful dish perfect for a quick and healthy meal. The combination of creamy avocado, crunchy corn, and hearty black beans, seasoned with lime and chili, creates a delicious filling that's both satisfying and nutritious. These tacos are highly customizable; feel free to add your favorite toppings or swap out ingredients to suit your taste. This recipe is a great way to enjoy a meatless meal without sacrificing flavor or texture. Whether you're hosting a taco night or looking for an easy weeknight dinner, these tacos are sure to please everyone at the table. Enjoy the burst of flavors and textures in every bite!

Sweet Potato and Kale Buddha Bowl

Ingredients:

- 2 large sweet potatoes, peeled and cubed
- 1 tablespoon olive oil
- Salt and freshly ground black pepper, to taste
- 4 cups kale, stems removed and leaves chopped
- 1 can (15 ounces) chickpeas, drained, rinsed, and dried
- 1 teaspoon smoked paprika
- 1 avocado, sliced
- 1/2 cup quinoa, rinsed
- 1 cup water or vegetable broth

For the Dressing:
- 3 tablespoons tahini
- 1 tablespoon maple syrup
- 1 tablespoon lemon juice
- Water, as needed to thin
- Optional toppings: pumpkin seeds, sliced radishes, sesame seeds

Instructions:

1. **Roast Sweet Potatoes:** Preheat oven to 400°F (200°C). Toss sweet potatoes with olive oil, salt, and pepper. Spread on a baking sheet and roast for 25-30 minutes, until tender and golden.
2. **Prepare Quinoa:** While sweet potatoes are roasting, combine quinoa and water (or broth) in a saucepan. Bring to a boil, reduce heat to low, cover, and simmer for 15 minutes, or until liquid is absorbed. Remove from heat and let stand covered for 5 minutes. Fluff with a fork.
3. **Cook Chickpeas:** Toss chickpeas with smoked paprika, salt, and a drizzle of olive oil. Spread on a baking sheet and roast in the oven with sweet potatoes for 20-25 minutes, until crispy.
4. **Sauté Kale:** In a large pan, heat a splash of olive oil over medium heat. Add kale and sauté until just wilted, about 3-5 minutes. Season with salt and pepper to taste.
5. **Prepare Dressing:** Whisk together tahini, maple syrup, and lemon juice in a small bowl. Add water, 1 tablespoon at a time, until desired consistency is reached.
6. **Assemble Buddha Bowls:** Divide quinoa among bowls. Top with roasted sweet potatoes, crispy chickpeas, sautéed kale, and avocado slices. Drizzle with tahini dressing and add optional toppings as desired.

Chef's Note:

The Sweet Potato and Kale Buddha Bowl is a nutrient-packed meal that's as satisfying as it is colorful. Combining the sweetness of roasted sweet potatoes with the earthiness of kale and the crunch of chickpeas, this bowl is a perfect balance of flavors and textures. The creamy tahini dressing adds a rich, nutty layer that ties everything together beautifully. This recipe is easily customizable with your favorite veggies or grains, making it a versatile option for any meal. Enjoy the vibrant colors and diverse nutrients packed into this delightful bowl, perfect for a health-conscious yet hearty meal.

Eggplant Parmesan Magic

Ingredients:

- 2 large eggplants, sliced into 1/2-inch rounds
- Salt, for drawing out moisture from eggplant
- 3 cups marinara sauce
- 2 cups all-purpose flour
- 4 eggs, beaten
- 3 cups breadcrumbs
- 1 tablespoon Italian seasoning
- 2 cups grated mozzarella cheese
- 1 cup grated Parmesan cheese
- Olive oil, for frying
- Fresh basil leaves, for garnish

Instructions:

1. Prep Eggplant: Sprinkle salt on both sides of the eggplant slices and let them sit for about 30 minutes to draw out moisture. Pat dry with paper towels.
2. Bread Eggplant: Dredge each eggplant slice in flour, dip in beaten eggs, and then coat in breadcrumbs mixed with Italian seasoning.
3. Fry Eggplant: Heat olive oil in a large skillet over medium heat. Fry the eggplant slices in batches until golden brown on both sides. Drain on paper towels.
4. Layer the Dish: Preheat the oven to 375°F (190°C). Spread a thin layer of marinara sauce on the bottom of a baking dish. Layer eggplant slices over the sauce, then top with more sauce, mozzarella, and Parmesan cheese. Repeat layers until all ingredients are used, finishing with cheese on top.
5. Bake: Bake for 25-30 minutes, or until the cheese is bubbly and golden brown.
6. Serve: Let the Eggplant Parmesan rest for a few minutes before serving. Garnish with fresh basil leaves.

Chef's Note:

Eggplant Parmesan Magic transforms simple ingredients into a sumptuous, comforting dish that's perfect for family dinners or special occasions. This recipe celebrates the rich flavors and textures of eggplant, marinara sauce, and melted cheeses, all layered together and baked to perfection. Drawing out the moisture from the eggplant ensures a crispy, not soggy, texture once fried. Serving this dish is like unveiling a piece of culinary magic, where each layer contributes to an overall harmony of taste. Enjoy the delightful blend of crispy eggplant, tangy tomato sauce, and gooey cheese, all enhanced by the fresh aroma of basil.

Crispy Cauliflower Buffalo Wings

Ingredients:

- 1 head of cauliflower, cut into bite-sized florets
- 1 cup all-purpose flour
- 1 cup water
- 1 teaspoon garlic powder
- 1/2 teaspoon salt
- 1/2 teaspoon paprika
- 2 cups breadcrumbs
- 3/4 cup buffalo sauce
- 2 tablespoons unsalted butter, melted (use vegan butter for a vegan version)
- Ranch or blue cheese dressing, for serving (use vegan alternatives for a vegan version)
- Celery sticks, for serving

Instructions:

1. Preheat Oven and Prepare Baking Sheet: Preheat your oven to 425°F (220°C). Line a baking sheet with parchment paper.
2. Make the Batter: In a large bowl, whisk together the flour, water, garlic powder, salt, and paprika until smooth. Dip each cauliflower floret into the batter, shaking off the excess.
3. Coat with Breadcrumbs: Roll the battered cauliflower in the breadcrumbs until evenly coated. Place on the prepared baking sheet.
4. Bake: Bake for 20-25 minutes, or until the cauliflower is crispy and golden brown.
5. Prepare Buffalo Sauce Mixture: While the cauliflower bakes, combine the buffalo sauce and melted butter in a large bowl.
6. Toss Cauliflower in Sauce: Remove the cauliflower from the oven and let it cool slightly. Toss the baked florets in the buffalo sauce mixture until well coated.
7. Bake Again: Return the coated cauliflower to the baking sheet and bake for an additional 10-15 minutes, or until crispy.
8. Serve: Serve the crispy cauliflower buffalo wings with ranch or blue cheese dressing and celery sticks on the side.

Chef's Note:

Crispy Cauliflower Buffalo Wings are a delightful, plant-based alternative to traditional chicken wings, offering all the spicy, tangy flavor of buffalo wings without the meat. This recipe is perfect for vegetarians, vegans, or anyone looking to incorporate more vegetables into their diet. The double-baking method ensures that the cauliflower is crispy on the outside and tender on the inside, making for a satisfying snack or appetizer. These "wings" are great for game day, parties, or as a tasty addition to any meal. Enjoy the bold flavors and satisfying crunch of these innovative cauliflower buffalo wings.

Snacks and Appetizers

This section of our cookbook celebrates the small interludes of pleasure between meals—the appetizers that tantalize the palate for a great dining experience and the snacks that just add conversation.

From the crispy, salty, and utterly irresistible to the light, refreshing, and tantalizingly sweet—this is the collection of nibbles that weaves the art of small bites. The recipes are such that it may cater to a grand party or else to one that precedes a family dinner, most essentially, also for that afternoon craving of something to eat, which will be both perfect and filling.

Join us in a culinary adventure where the appetizers are not just a course but a carnival of flavors and an epitome of fusion.

Garlicky Parmesan Zucchini Bites

Ingredients:

- 2 medium zucchinis, sliced into 1/4-inch rounds
- 2 tablespoons olive oil
- 3 cloves garlic, minced
- Salt and freshly ground black pepper, to taste
- 1/2 cup grated Parmesan cheese
- 1/4 cup breadcrumbs
- 1 teaspoon Italian seasoning
- Fresh parsley, chopped, for garnish

Instructions:

1. Preheat Oven and Prepare Baking Sheet: Preheat your oven to 425°F (220°C). Line a baking sheet with parchment paper or lightly grease it.
2. Season Zucchini: In a large bowl, toss the zucchini rounds with olive oil, minced garlic, salt, and pepper until evenly coated.
3. Combine Parmesan and Breadcrumbs: In a small bowl, mix together the grated Parmesan, breadcrumbs, and Italian seasoning.
4. Coat Zucchini: Dip each zucchini round into the Parmesan mixture, pressing the mixture onto both sides of the zucchini. Place the coated zucchini rounds in a single layer on the prepared baking sheet.
5. Bake: Bake in the preheated oven for about 15-20 minutes, or until the zucchini is tender and the coating is crispy and golden brown.
6. Garnish and Serve: Garnish the baked zucchini bites with chopped fresh parsley before serving.

Chef's Note:

Garlicky Parmesan Zucchini Bites are a simple, delicious appetizer or snack that's perfect for satisfying your savory cravings. The combination of garlic and Parmesan creates a flavorful crust that complements the tender zucchini, while the Italian seasoning adds an extra layer of herbaceous notes. These bites are not only easy to prepare but also a healthier alternative to traditional fried appetizers. They're great for parties, gatherings, or just a fun way to get your veggies in. Serve them hot out of the oven for the best taste and texture, and watch them disappear in no time!

Crisp Honey Sriracha Chicken Wings

Ingredients:

- 2 pounds chicken wings, tips removed, drumettes and flats separated
- Salt and freshly ground black pepper, to taste
- 1 tablespoon baking powder (NOT baking soda)
- 1/4 cup honey
- 1/4 cup Sriracha sauce
- 2 tablespoons soy sauce
- 1 tablespoon rice vinegar
- 1 clove garlic, minced
- 1 teaspoon ginger, grated
- Sesame seeds, for garnish
- Green onions, thinly sliced, for garnish

Instructions:

1. Prepare Chicken Wings: Pat the chicken wings dry with paper towels. Season with salt and pepper. Toss the wings with baking powder to coat evenly. This helps to make the skin super crispy.
2. Bake Wings: Preheat your oven to 425°F (220°C). Line a baking sheet with aluminum foil and place a wire rack on top. Arrange the wings on the rack in a single layer. Bake for 45-50 minutes, or until the wings are golden and crispy, flipping halfway through the cooking time.
3. Make Honey Sriracha Sauce: While the wings are baking, combine honey, Sriracha sauce, soy sauce, rice vinegar, garlic, and ginger in a small saucepan over medium heat. Bring to a simmer and cook until slightly thickened, about 5 minutes. Remove from heat.
4. Toss Wings in Sauce: Once the wings are cooked, transfer them to a large bowl. Pour the Honey Sriracha sauce over the wings and toss to coat evenly.
5. Serve: Garnish the wings with sesame seeds and sliced green onions. Serve immediately.

Chef's Note:

Crisp Honey Sriracha Chicken Wings are the perfect blend of sweet, spicy, and savory, making them an irresistible appetizer or snack for any occasion. The secret to achieving the ultimate crispiness lies in the use of baking powder, which draws moisture out of the skin. The Honey Sriracha sauce provides a tantalizing glaze that clings to each wing, delivering a burst of flavor in every bite. These wings are sure to be a hit at parties, game days, or during a casual dinner at home. Enjoy the delightful contrast of textures and flavors that make this dish a crowd-pleaser.

Smoked Salmon Cucumber Rolls

Ingredients:

- 2 large cucumbers
- 8 ounces smoked salmon, thinly sliced
- 4 ounces cream cheese, softened (use dairy-free for a vegan version)
- 1 tablespoon fresh dill, chopped, plus extra for garnish
- 1 tablespoon lemon juice
- Salt and freshly ground black pepper, to taste
- Optional: capers for garnish

Instructions:

1. **Prepare Cucumbers:** Using a vegetable peeler or mandoline, slice the cucumbers lengthwise into thin strips.
2. **Mix Filling:** In a small bowl, combine the cream cheese, chopped dill, lemon juice, salt, and pepper. Mix until smooth and well combined.
3. **Assemble Rolls:** Lay a slice of smoked salmon on top of each cucumber strip. Spread a thin layer of the cream cheese mixture over the salmon. Carefully roll up the cucumber slices tightly.
4. **Serve:** Arrange the cucumber rolls on a serving platter. Garnish with additional dill and capers if desired.

Chef's Note:

Smoked Salmon Cucumber Rolls are a refreshing and elegant appetizer perfect for any gathering or special occasion. The crispness of the cucumber paired with the rich flavor of smoked salmon and the creamy dill-infused cream cheese makes for a delightful combination of textures and tastes. These rolls are not only visually appealing but also light and healthy, making them an excellent choice for those looking for a sophisticated yet simple-to-prepare snack. For a dairy-free or vegan version, substitute the cream cheese with your favorite plant-based alternative. Enjoy the burst of fresh flavors with each bite of these delightful cucumber rolls.

Mini Caprese Skewers with Balsamic Glaze

Ingredients:

- 24 cherry tomatoes
- 24 small mozzarella balls (bocconcini)
- 24 fresh basil leaves
- 24 toothpicks or small skewers
- 1/2 cup balsamic vinegar
- 2 tablespoons honey
- Salt and freshly ground black pepper, to taste
- Olive oil, for drizzling

Instructions:

1. Prepare Balsamic Glaze: In a small saucepan over medium heat, combine balsamic vinegar and honey. Bring to a simmer and reduce by half, or until the mixture thickens into a glaze, about 10-15 minutes. Set aside to cool.
2. Assemble Skewers: Thread one cherry tomato, one basil leaf (folded if large), and one mozzarella ball onto each toothpick or skewer.
3. Season: Lightly season the skewers with salt and pepper, and drizzle with olive oil.
4. Serve with Glaze: Arrange the skewers on a serving platter and drizzle with the balsamic glaze just before serving.

Chef's Note:

Mini Caprese Skewers with Balsamic Glaze are a delightful, easy-to-make appetizer that captures the essence of classic Caprese salad in a bite-sized, party-friendly format. The combination of juicy cherry tomatoes, creamy mozzarella, and fresh basil, enhanced by the sweet and tangy balsamic glaze, creates a harmonious blend of flavors and textures. These skewers are perfect for entertaining, offering a visually appealing and mess-free option for guests to enjoy. The homemade balsamic glaze adds a gourmet touch that elevates this simple dish into a memorable culinary experience. Enjoy the elegance and simplicity of these skewers at your next gathering!

Savory Spinach and Feta Puff Pastries

Ingredients:

- 1 sheet puff pastry, thawed
- 2 cups fresh spinach, chopped
- 1 cup feta cheese, crumbled
- 1/2 cup ricotta cheese
- 1 egg, beaten (for egg wash)
- 2 tablespoons olive oil
- 2 cloves garlic, minced
- Salt and freshly ground black pepper, to taste
- Sesame seeds, for garnish (optional)

Instructions:

1. **Preheat Oven and Prepare Pastry:** Preheat your oven to 400°F (200°C). Roll out the puff pastry on a lightly floured surface and cut into squares or rectangles, depending on your preference.
2. **Sauté Spinach:** Heat olive oil in a skillet over medium heat. Add garlic and sauté for 1 minute. Add the spinach and cook until wilted, about 3-4 minutes. Season with salt and pepper. Let cool.
3. **Mix Filling:** In a bowl, combine the sautéed spinach, feta cheese, and ricotta cheese. Mix well.
4. **Assemble Pastries:** Spoon a portion of the spinach and cheese mixture onto the center of each puff pastry square. Fold the pastry over the filling to create a triangle or rectangle, pressing the edges to seal. Use a fork to crimp the edges for extra security.
5. **Apply Egg Wash:** Brush the top of each pastry with beaten egg and sprinkle with sesame seeds if using.
6. **Bake:** Place the pastries on a baking sheet lined with parchment paper. Bake for 15-20 minutes, or until the pastries are golden brown and puffed.
7. **Serve:** Allow to cool slightly before serving.

Chef's Note:

Savory Spinach and Feta Puff Pastries are a delightful treat that combines the creamy, tangy flavors of feta and ricotta cheeses with the freshness of spinach, all encased in flaky, buttery puff pastry. This recipe is perfect for appetizers, brunch, or even as a light meal. The combination of ingredients can be adjusted to suit your taste, making it versatile and suitable for various occasions. The key to success is not overfilling the pastries to ensure they seal properly and puff beautifully. Enjoy the elegant simplicity of these pastries, which are sure to impress guests and satisfy your savory cravings.

Sweet Potato Rounds with Goat Cheese and Cranberry

Ingredients:

- 2 large sweet potatoes, sliced into 1/4-inch rounds
- 2 tablespoons olive oil
- Salt and freshly ground black pepper, to taste
- 1 cup goat cheese, softened
- 1/2 cup dried cranberries
- 1/4 cup pecans, chopped (optional)
- Honey, for drizzling
- Fresh thyme leaves, for garnish

Instructions:

1. **Preheat Oven and Prepare Sweet Potatoes:** Preheat your oven to 425°F (220°C). Toss the sweet potato rounds with olive oil, salt, and pepper. Arrange them in a single layer on a baking sheet lined with parchment paper.
2. **Bake:** Bake for 20-25 minutes, flipping halfway through, until the sweet potatoes are tender and slightly golden around the edges.
3. **Assemble Rounds:** Once the sweet potato rounds have cooled slightly, top each round with a dollop of goat cheese, followed by a sprinkling of dried cranberries and chopped pecans, if using.
4. **Final Touches:** Drizzle honey over the assembled sweet potato rounds and garnish with fresh thyme leaves.
5. **Serve:** Serve immediately as a warm appetizer or a delightful snack.

Chef's Note:

Sweet Potato Rounds with Goat Cheese and Cranberry offer a harmonious blend of sweet, savory, and tart flavors, all in one bite-sized appetizer. This recipe is a testament to the versatility of sweet potatoes, complemented by the creamy tanginess of goat cheese and the chewy sweetness of cranberries. The addition of pecans introduces a crunchy texture and nutty flavor, while a drizzle of honey and a sprinkle of fresh thyme elevate the dish with a hint of sweetness and a fresh herbal note. These rounds are perfect for holiday gatherings, parties, or as an elegant snack. Enjoy the delightful contrast of flavors and textures that make this dish a crowd-pleaser.

Baked Avocado Fries with Chipotle Aioli

Ingredients:

- 2 ripe avocados, peeled, pitted, and sliced into wedges
- 1/2 cup flour
- 1 teaspoon salt
- 1/2 teaspoon black pepper
- 2 eggs, beaten
- 1 cup panko breadcrumbs
- 1 teaspoon garlic powder
- 1/2 teaspoon paprika
- Cooking spray

For the Chipotle Aioli:

- 1/2 cup mayonnaise (use vegan mayonnaise for a vegan version)
- 1 chipotle pepper in adobo sauce, minced
- 1 tablespoon adobo sauce (from the can of chipotle peppers)
- 1 clove garlic, minced
- Juice of 1 lime

Instructions:

1. **Preheat Oven and Prepare Baking Sheet:** Preheat your oven to 400°F (200°C). Line a baking sheet with parchment paper and lightly spray with cooking spray.
2. **Prepare Avocado Wedges:** Season the flour with salt and pepper. Dredge the avocado slices in the seasoned flour, then dip them in the beaten eggs, and finally coat them in a mixture of panko breadcrumbs, garlic powder, and paprika.
3. **Bake:** Place the coated avocado slices on the prepared baking sheet in a single layer. Spray the tops lightly with cooking spray. Bake for 15-20 minutes, or until the breadcrumbs are golden brown and crispy, flipping halfway through.
4. **Make Chipotle Aioli:** While the avocado fries are baking, mix together mayonnaise, chipotle pepper, adobo sauce, minced garlic, and lime juice in a small bowl. Adjust seasoning to taste.
5. **Serve:** Serve the baked avocado fries immediately with the chipotle aioli for dipping.

Chef's Note:

Baked Avocado Fries with Chipotle Aioli offer a unique twist on traditional fries, providing a creamy inside with a crispy, flavorful outside. The combination of the mild, buttery avocado with the spicy, tangy aioli creates a delightful contrast that's hard to resist. This dish serves as a perfect appetizer, snack, or side, offering a healthier alternative to deep-fried options without compromising on taste. The chipotle aioli, with its smoky depth and zesty lime kick, complements the avocado fries perfectly, making for a memorable and savory treat. Enjoy this easy-to-make, crowd-pleasing recipe that's sure to add a creative touch to any meal.

Spicy Roasted Chickpeas

Ingredients:

- 2 cans (15 ounces each) chickpeas, drained, rinsed, and thoroughly dried
- 2 tablespoons olive oil
- 1 teaspoon smoked paprika
- 1/2 teaspoon garlic powder
- 1/2 teaspoon cayenne pepper (adjust to taste)
- 1/2 teaspoon ground cumin
- Salt and freshly ground black pepper, to taste

Instructions:

1. Preheat Oven: Preheat your oven to 400°F (200°C). Line a baking sheet with parchment paper.
2. Season Chickpeas: In a large bowl, toss the dried chickpeas with olive oil, smoked paprika, garlic powder, cayenne pepper, ground cumin, salt, and black pepper until evenly coated.
3. Roast: Spread the chickpeas in a single layer on the prepared baking sheet. Roast for 25-30 minutes, stirring occasionally, until crispy and golden brown.
4. Cool: Allow the chickpeas to cool on the baking sheet for a few minutes; they will continue to crisp up as they cool.
5. Serve: Enjoy the spicy roasted chickpeas as a crunchy, flavorful snack or appetizer.

Chef's Note:

Spicy Roasted Chickpeas are a delightful and healthy alternative to traditional snacks. Packed with protein and fiber, these chickpeas offer a satisfying crunch with a kick of spice that's hard to resist. The combination of smoked paprika, garlic, cayenne, and cumin provides a robust flavor profile that makes these chickpeas a versatile snack. They're perfect for serving at parties, as a crispy salad topping, or for munching on throughout the day. Adjust the level of spice to suit your taste and experiment with other seasonings to create your own unique version. Enjoy this simple, nutritious snack that's as fun to make as it is to eat!

Prosciutto-Wrapped Asparagus Spears

Ingredients:

- 16 asparagus spears, tough ends trimmed
- 8 slices of prosciutto, halved lengthwise
- 1 tablespoon olive oil
- Salt and freshly ground black pepper, to taste
- Grated Parmesan cheese, for garnish (optional)
- Balsamic glaze, for drizzling (optional)

Instructions:

1. Preheat Oven: Preheat your oven to 400°F (200°C). Line a baking sheet with parchment paper.
2. Prepare Asparagus: Lightly toss the asparagus spears in olive oil, salt, and pepper.
3. Wrap Asparagus: Wrap each asparagus spear with a half slice of prosciutto, starting from the bottom and spiraling up to just below the tip.
4. Bake: Arrange the wrapped asparagus spears on the prepared baking sheet. Bake for 12-15 minutes, or until the asparagus is tender and the prosciutto is crisp.
5. Garnish and Serve: Transfer the prosciutto-wrapped asparagus to a serving platter. Sprinkle with grated Parmesan cheese and drizzle with balsamic glaze if desired.

Chef's Note:

Prosciutto-Wrapped Asparagus Spears are an elegant and simple appetizer that combines the savory flavor of prosciutto with the fresh, green crunch of asparagus. This dish is perfect for entertaining, offering a sophisticated yet easy-to-prepare option that's sure to impress your guests. The saltiness of the prosciutto perfectly complements the natural sweetness of the asparagus, while a drizzle of balsamic glaze adds a touch of acidity and sweetness to balance the flavors. Garnishing with Parmesan cheese adds an extra layer of umami, making each bite a delightful experience. Whether served as a starter or a side, these spears are a delicious way to elevate your meal.

Cheesy Garlic Breadsticks

Ingredients:

- 1 pound pizza dough, room temperature
- 4 tablespoons unsalted butter, melted
- 3 cloves garlic, minced
- 1 teaspoon Italian seasoning
- 1/2 teaspoon salt
- 1/4 teaspoon black pepper
- 1 cup shredded mozzarella cheese
- 1/4 cup grated Parmesan cheese
- Marinara sauce, for dipping

Instructions:

1. Preheat Oven and Prepare Baking Sheet: Preheat your oven to 425°F (220°C). Line a baking sheet with parchment paper or lightly grease it.
2. Roll Out Dough: On a lightly floured surface, roll out the pizza dough into a rectangle about 1/2 inch thick. Transfer the dough to the prepared baking sheet.
3. Prepare Garlic Butter: In a small bowl, mix together the melted butter, minced garlic, Italian seasoning, salt, and pepper.
4. Apply Garlic Butter: Brush the garlic butter mixture evenly over the top of the dough.
5. Add Cheese: Sprinkle the shredded mozzarella and grated Parmesan cheese evenly over the garlic butter.
6. Bake: Bake in the preheated oven for 12-15 minutes, or until the cheese is melted and bubbly and the edges of the dough are golden brown.
7. Cut and Serve: Remove from the oven and let cool for a couple of minutes. Cut into strips and serve warm with marinara sauce for dipping.

Chef's Note:

Cheesy Garlic Breadsticks are the perfect blend of crispy, gooey, and garlicky goodness, making them an irresistible appetizer or side dish. The key to achieving the perfect texture is to roll the dough to the right thickness and to bake until just golden for that delightful crunch. The combination of mozzarella and Parmesan provides a rich, cheesy flavor that complements the garlicky butter beautifully. These breadsticks are great for sharing and are sure to be a hit at any gathering. Serve them alongside your favorite pasta dish, soup, or salad, or enjoy them on their own with a side of marinara sauce for the ultimate treat.

Desserts

Desserts: the grand finale to any meal, where sweetness and creativity come together to create moments of pure delight.

This section deals with the art of making sweets - everything from the most accustomed to revamped—modern favorites. Whether you're looking for a sinfully rich chocolate cake, bright and fruity tarts, or even something all your own, these recipes are really meant to help satisfy that sweet tooth in you and get your culinary imagination rolling in the kitchen.

Enter a world where sugar, spice, and everything nice make an unforgettable end to your culinary adventure. Indulge in these sweet creations which will tempt, indulge, and inspire.

Decadent Chocolate Lava Cakes

Ingredients:

- 6 ounces semisweet chocolate, chopped
- 1/2 cup (1 stick) unsalted butter
- 1 cup powdered sugar
- 2 large eggs
- 2 large egg yolks
- 1 teaspoon vanilla extract
- 1/3 cup all-purpose flour
- Pinch of salt
- Cocoa powder or powdered sugar, for dusting
- Fresh berries or whipped cream, for serving (optional)

Instructions:

1. **Preheat Oven:** Preheat your oven to 425°F (220°C). Grease four 6-ounce ramekins with butter or non-stick spray.
2. **Melt Chocolate and Butter:** In a medium heatproof bowl, melt the chocolate and butter together in the microwave in 30-second bursts, stirring after each burst, until smooth and combined.
3. **Mix Ingredients:** Whisk in the powdered sugar until well blended. Add the eggs and egg yolks, one at a time, whisking after each addition. Stir in the vanilla extract. Gently fold in the flour and a pinch of salt until just combined.
4. **Fill Ramekins:** Divide the batter evenly among the prepared ramekins.
5. **Bake:** Bake for 12-14 minutes, or until the edges are firm but the center is still soft.
6. **Serve:** Let the cakes rest for 1 minute, then invert onto plates. Dust with cocoa powder or powdered sugar. Serve immediately with fresh berries or whipped cream if desired.

Chef's Note:

Decadent Chocolate Lava Cakes are the epitome of indulgent desserts, combining a rich chocolate flavor with a gooey, molten center that oozes out with the first bite. The key to achieving the perfect lava texture is to not overbake the cakes, as the center should remain soft and flowing. These cakes are surprisingly easy to make and are sure to impress guests or provide a luxurious treat for a special occasion. Enjoy the warm, comforting taste of these lava cakes, and feel free to customize with your favorite toppings or accompaniments.

Classic Vanilla Bean Panna Cotta

Ingredients:

- 2 cups heavy cream
- 1 vanilla bean, split lengthwise and seeds scraped
- 1/2 cup granulated sugar
- 1 1/2 teaspoons gelatin powder
- 3 tablespoons cold water
- 1 cup whole milk
- Fresh berries or berry sauce, for serving

Instructions:

1. **Bloom Gelatin:** In a small bowl, sprinkle the gelatin over the cold water. Let it stand for about 5 to 10 minutes, or until the gelatin has softened.
2. **Heat Cream and Vanilla:** In a saucepan, combine the heavy cream, granulated sugar, vanilla bean seeds, and the pod. Heat over medium heat, stirring constantly, until the sugar has dissolved. Do not let it boil.
3. **Dissolve Gelatin:** Remove the cream mixture from the heat. Remove the vanilla bean pod. Add the softened gelatin to the cream mixture and stir until the gelatin is completely dissolved.
4. **Add Milk:** Stir in the whole milk until well combined.
5. **Pour into Molds:** Divide the mixture among serving glasses or ramekins. Refrigerate for at least 4 hours, or until set.
6. **Serve:** Once set, serve the panna cotta with fresh berries or a berry sauce.

Chef's Note:

Classic Vanilla Bean Panna Cotta is an elegant, smooth dessert that's surprisingly simple to make. The key to its delicate texture lies in the balance between the gelatin and the creamy mixture. Using a real vanilla bean not only infuses the panna cotta with a rich, authentic flavor but also adds those beautiful specks of vanilla seeds throughout the dessert. This dish is perfect for impressing guests or enjoying a luxurious treat at home. The panna cotta can be made ahead of time, making it an excellent choice for dinner parties. Serve it with fresh berries or a berry sauce for a refreshing contrast to the creamy texture.

Easy Mixed Berry Crumble

Ingredients:

- **For the Berry Filling:**
- 4 cups mixed berries (fresh or frozen and thawed)
- 1/2 cup granulated sugar
- 2 tablespoons cornstarch
- Juice of 1 lemon

- **For the Crumble Topping:**
- 3/4 cup all-purpose flour
- 1/2 cup rolled oats
- 1/2 cup light brown sugar, packed
- 1/2 teaspoon cinnamon
- 1/4 teaspoon salt
- 1/2 cup unsalted butter, cold and cubed

Instructions:

1. Preheat Oven: Preheat your oven to 375°F (190°C).
2. Prepare Berry Filling: In a large bowl, combine the mixed berries, granulated sugar, cornstarch, and lemon juice. Gently toss to coat the berries evenly. Pour the berry mixture into an 8x8-inch baking dish.
3. Make Crumble Topping: In another bowl, mix together the flour, oats, brown sugar, cinnamon, and salt. Add the cubed butter and use your fingers or a pastry cutter to work the butter into the dry ingredients until the mixture resembles coarse crumbs.
4. Assemble and Bake: Sprinkle the crumble topping evenly over the berry filling. Bake for 35-40 minutes, or until the topping is golden brown and the berry filling is bubbling.
5. Serve: Let the crumble cool slightly before serving. Enjoy warm, optionally with a scoop of vanilla ice cream or a dollop of whipped cream.

Chef's Note:

This Easy Mixed Berry Crumble is the perfect dessert for any season, offering a delightful combination of sweet and tart flavors from the berries, topped with a crispy, buttery crumble. Using a mix of berries provides a beautiful variety of flavors and colors, but feel free to use any combination of berries you prefer or have on hand. The crumble is wonderfully versatile and can be easily adapted to include nuts or spices according to your taste. It's a simple yet impressive dessert that's sure to please a crowd, whether it's for a cozy family dinner or a festive gathering.

No-Bake Lemon Cheesecake Cups

Ingredients:

- **For the Crust:**
  - 1 cup graham cracker crumbs
  - 4 tablespoons unsalted butter, melted
  - 2 tablespoons granulated sugar

- **For the Cheesecake Filling:**
  - 1 package (8 ounces) cream cheese, softened
  - 1 can (14 ounces) sweetened condensed milk
  - 1/3 cup fresh lemon juice
  - 1 teaspoon lemon zest
  - 1 teaspoon vanilla extract

- **For Garnish:**
  - Whipped cream
  - Additional lemon zest
  - Fresh berries

Instructions:

1. **Prepare Crust:** In a bowl, mix together graham cracker crumbs, melted butter, and sugar until well combined. Press the mixture into the bottom of individual serving cups or glasses, creating a firm base. Chill in the refrigerator while preparing the filling.
2. **Make Cheesecake Filling:** In a large bowl, use an electric mixer to beat the cream cheese until smooth. Gradually add the sweetened condensed milk, beating until well blended. Mix in the lemon juice, lemon zest, and vanilla extract until the mixture is smooth and creamy.
3. **Assemble Cheesecake Cups:** Spoon the cheesecake filling over the crust in each cup, smoothing the tops with a spoon or spatula. Refrigerate for at least 3 hours, or until set.
4. **Garnish and Serve:** Before serving, top each cheesecake cup with whipped cream, a sprinkle of lemon zest, and fresh berries.

Chef's Note:

No-Bake Lemon Cheesecake Cups are a delightfully refreshing and easy-to-make dessert that's perfect for any occasion. The combination of tangy lemon and creamy cheesecake filling, atop a buttery graham cracker crust, offers a balance of flavors and textures that's sure to please. These individual servings not only make for a beautiful presentation but also add a personal touch to your dessert offering. The no-bake aspect makes this recipe ideal for warm weather or whenever you want a delicious dessert without turning on the oven. Enjoy these lemon cheesecake cups as a sweet, citrusy treat that's bound to impress.

Fluffy Red Velvet Cupcakes

Ingredients:

- **For the Cupcakes:**
- 1 1/4 cups all-purpose flour
- 1/2 cup granulated sugar
- 1/2 teaspoon baking soda
- 1/2 teaspoon salt
- 1 tablespoon cocoa powder
- 3/4 cup vegetable oil
- 1/2 cup buttermilk, at room temperature
- 1 large egg, at room temperature
- 2 tablespoons red food coloring
- 1 teaspoon white vinegar
- 1 teaspoon vanilla extract

- **For the Cream Cheese Frosting:**
- 8 ounces cream cheese, softened
- 1/2 cup unsalted butter, softened
- 3 cups powdered sugar, sifted
- 1 teaspoon vanilla extract

Instructions:

1. Preheat Oven and Prepare Pan: Preheat your oven to 350°F (175°C). Line a muffin tin with cupcake liners.
2. Mix Dry Ingredients: In a medium bowl, whisk together the flour, sugar, baking soda, salt, and cocoa powder.
3. Combine Wet Ingredients: In a large bowl, mix the vegetable oil, buttermilk, egg, red food coloring, white vinegar, and vanilla extract until well combined.
4. Combine Wet and Dry Ingredients: Add the dry ingredients to the wet ingredients, mixing until just combined. Be careful not to overmix.
5. Fill Cupcake Liners: Divide the batter evenly among the cupcake liners, filling each about 2/3 full.
6. Bake: Bake for 18-20 minutes, or until a toothpick inserted into the center comes out clean. Allow cupcakes to cool in the pan for 5 minutes, then transfer to a wire rack to cool completely.
7. Make Frosting: Beat the cream cheese and butter together until smooth. Gradually add the powdered sugar and vanilla extract, beating until creamy and smooth.
8. Frost Cupcakes: Once the cupcakes are completely cooled, frost them with the cream cheese frosting.
9. Serve: Enjoy your fluffy red velvet cupcakes as is or garnish with red sprinkles or fresh berries for an extra touch.

Chef's Note:

Fluffy Red Velvet Cupcakes are a classic treat that combines the rich flavors of cocoa with a slight tang from buttermilk and cream cheese frosting. The key to their signature fluffy texture lies in not overmixing the batter and the use of buttermilk and vinegar, which react with the baking soda to create a tender crumb. The vibrant red color makes these cupcakes a stunning addition to any celebration or gathering. Enjoy the delightful contrast between the moist, flavorful cake and the creamy, rich frosting.

Cinnamon Apple Galette

Ingredients:

- **For the Pastry:**
- 1 1/4 cups all-purpose flour
- 1/2 teaspoon salt
- 1 teaspoon sugar
- 1/2 cup (1 stick) unsalted butter, cold and cubed
- 1/4 cup ice water

- **For the Filling:**
- 3 medium apples, peeled, cored, and thinly sliced
- 1/4 cup granulated sugar
- 1 teaspoon ground cinnamon
- 1 tablespoon all-purpose flour
- 1 tablespoon unsalted butter, melted
- 1 egg, beaten (for egg wash)
- Turbinado sugar, for sprinkling (optional)

Instructions:

1. Make the Pastry Dough: In a large bowl, combine flour, salt, and sugar. Add the cold, cubed butter and use a pastry cutter or your fingers to mix until the mixture resembles coarse crumbs. Gradually add ice water, stirring until the dough just comes together. Form into a disk, wrap in plastic wrap, and chill for at least 1 hour.
2. Preheat Oven: Preheat your oven to 375°F (190°C).
3. Prepare Apples: In a bowl, toss the sliced apples with sugar, cinnamon, and flour until evenly coated.
4. Roll Out Dough: On a lightly floured surface, roll out the chilled dough into a 12-inch circle. Transfer to a baking sheet lined with parchment paper.
5. Assemble Galette: Arrange the apple slices in the center of the dough, leaving a 2-inch border. Fold the edges of the dough over the apples, pleating as needed. Brush the dough with melted butter and the egg wash. Sprinkle with turbinado sugar if using.
6. Bake: Bake for 35-40 minutes, or until the crust is golden brown and the apples are tender.
7. Serve: Let the galette cool slightly before slicing. Serve warm or at room temperature.

Chef's Note:

The Cinnamon Apple Galette is a rustic, free-form tart that combines the simplicity of a homemade crust with the warm, comforting flavors of cinnamon and apple. Its beauty lies in its imperfections, making it a forgiving recipe for bakers of all levels. The galette is perfect for when you crave something sweet but want to keep things simple. The flaky pastry and spiced apple filling make it an ideal dessert for cozy autumn evenings, served with a dollop of whipped cream or a scoop of vanilla ice cream. Enjoy the delightful blend of textures and flavors in this timeless treat.

Quick Chocolate Chip Cookie Bars

Ingredients:

- 2 1/4 cups all-purpose flour
- 1/2 teaspoon baking soda
- 1/2 teaspoon salt
- 3/4 cup unsalted butter, melted
- 1 cup packed brown sugar
- 1/2 cup granulated sugar
- 1 tablespoon vanilla extract
- 2 large eggs
- 2 cups semisweet chocolate chips
- Optional: 1 cup chopped nuts (walnuts or pecans)

Instructions:

1. **Preheat Oven and Prepare Pan:** Preheat your oven to 350°F (175°C). Line a 9x13-inch baking pan with parchment paper, leaving an overhang on the sides to lift the bars out easily after baking.
2. **Mix Dry Ingredients:** In a medium bowl, whisk together the flour, baking soda, and salt. Set aside.
3. **Combine Butter and Sugars:** In a large bowl, mix the melted butter, brown sugar, and granulated sugar until well combined. Beat in the vanilla extract and eggs, one at a time, until the mixture is light and creamy.
4. **Add Dry Ingredients:** Gradually blend the dry ingredients into the wet mixture, stirring just until combined. Fold in the chocolate chips and optional nuts.
5. **Spread in Pan:** Spread the cookie dough evenly in the prepared pan, smoothing the top with a spatula.
6. **Bake:** Bake for 25-30 minutes, or until the top is golden brown and a toothpick inserted into the center comes out clean. Be careful not to overbake.
7. **Cool and Cut:** Let the bars cool completely in the pan set on a wire rack. Once cool, use the parchment paper overhang to lift the bars out of the pan. Cut into squares or rectangles.

Chef's Note:

Quick Chocolate Chip Cookie Bars are a delightful twist on the classic chocolate chip cookie, offering all the chewy goodness in a convenient bar form. This recipe is perfect for when you're short on time but craving something sweet and homemade. The melted butter gives these bars a wonderfully soft and chewy texture, while the combination of brown and granulated sugars adds depth to the flavor. These bars are versatile and can be customized with your favorite add-ins, such as nuts or different types of chocolate chips. Whether you're baking for a crowd, a family dessert, or simply treating yourself, these cookie bars are sure to satisfy any sweet tooth.

Peaches and Cream Tartlets

Ingredients:

- **For the Tartlet Shells:**
- 1 1/4 cups all-purpose flour
- 1/4 teaspoon salt
- 1/2 cup unsalted butter, cold and cubed
- 2-3 tablespoons ice water

- **For the Filling:**
- 1 cup heavy cream
- 2 tablespoons powdered sugar
- 1/2 teaspoon vanilla extract
- 2 large peaches, sliced thin
- Honey, for drizzling (optional)
- Mint leaves, for garnish (optional)

Instructions:

1. Prepare Tartlet Shells: In a food processor, pulse the flour and salt. Add the butter and pulse until the mixture resembles coarse crumbs. Gradually add ice water, 1 tablespoon at a time, until the dough just comes together. Form into a disk, wrap in plastic, and chill for 30 minutes.
2. Roll and Bake Shells: Preheat the oven to 375°F (190°C). On a floured surface, roll out the dough and cut into rounds to fit tartlet pans. Press the dough into the pans and prick the bottoms with a fork. Bake for 12-15 minutes or until golden. Let cool.
3. Whip the Cream: Beat the heavy cream, powdered sugar, and vanilla extract until stiff peaks form.
4. Assemble Tartlets: Fill each cooled tartlet shell with whipped cream. Arrange peach slices on top. Drizzle with honey and garnish with mint leaves if desired.
5. Serve: Chill the tartlets for at least 1 hour before serving to allow the flavors to meld.

Chef's Note:

Peaches and Cream Tartlets are a delightful, elegant dessert perfect for summer gatherings or as a sweet finish to any meal. The combination of buttery crust, rich whipped cream, and fresh peaches celebrates the season's best flavors. These tartlets are not only visually appealing but also offer a burst of freshness with each bite. The optional drizzle of honey enhances the natural sweetness of the peaches, while mint leaves add a refreshing note. For the best results, use ripe, juicy peaches and serve the tartlets chilled. Enjoy the simplicity and sophistication of this timeless dessert.

Coconut Mango Sticky Rice

Ingredients:

- 1 cup glutinous (sticky) rice
- 1 can (14 ounces) coconut milk
- 1/2 cup granulated sugar
- 1/2 teaspoon salt
- 1 ripe mango, peeled and sliced
- Sesame seeds or toasted coconut flakes, for garnish
- Mint leaves, for garnish (optional)

Instructions:

1. Soak the Rice: Rinse the sticky rice under cold water until the water runs clear. Soak the rice in water for at least 1 hour, or overnight for best results. Drain thoroughly.
2. Cook the Rice: In a pot, combine the drained rice with enough water to cover it by about an inch. Bring to a boil, then reduce the heat to low, cover, and simmer for 10-15 minutes, or until the water is absorbed and the rice is tender. Remove from heat and let it sit, covered, for 10 minutes.
3. Prepare Coconut Sauce: In another pot, combine the coconut milk, granulated sugar, and salt. Warm over medium heat, stirring until the sugar is dissolved. Do not let it boil.
4. Mix Rice with Coconut Sauce: Reserve 1/4 cup of the coconut sauce for serving. Add the cooked rice to the remaining coconut sauce in the pot, stirring gently to combine. Cover and let the mixture sit for about 30 minutes to allow the rice to absorb the sauce.
5. Serve: Spoon the coconut mango sticky rice onto plates or into bowls. Top with fresh mango slices. Drizzle with the reserved coconut sauce and garnish with sesame seeds, toasted coconut flakes, or mint leaves.

Chef's Note:

Coconut Mango Sticky Rice is a classic Southeast Asian dessert that's both simple and delicious. The combination of sweet, sticky rice with creamy coconut and fresh mango creates a harmony of flavors and textures that's hard to resist. This dessert is traditionally served as a sweet finish to meals or as a snack during the day. For the best flavor and presentation, use ripe mangoes that are sweet and juicy. This dish is a wonderful way to bring a taste of the tropics to your table, offering a delightful and refreshing dessert option that's perfect for warm weather or whenever you crave something sweet and satisfying.

Rustic Pear and Almond Tart

Ingredients:

- **For the Crust:**
  - 1 1/4 cups all-purpose flour
  - 1/4 teaspoon salt
  - 1/2 cup (1 stick) unsalted butter, cold and cubed
  - 2-4 tablespoons ice water

- **For the Filling:**
  - 3 ripe pears, peeled, cored, and thinly sliced
  - 1/2 cup granulated sugar
  - 1 teaspoon vanilla extract
  - 1/2 teaspoon ground cinnamon
  - 1/4 cup almond flour

- **For the Topping:**
  - 1/4 cup sliced almonds
  - Powdered sugar, for dusting (optional)

Instructions:

1. **Prepare the Crust:** In a large bowl, mix the all-purpose flour and salt. Add the cold, cubed butter and work it into the flour using a pastry blender or your fingers until the mixture resembles coarse crumbs. Gradually add ice water, stirring until the dough comes together. Form into a disk, wrap in plastic, and chill for at least 30 minutes.
2. **Preheat Oven:** Preheat your oven to 375°F (190°C).
3. **Roll Out Dough:** On a lightly floured surface, roll out the dough into a 12-inch circle. Transfer to a baking sheet lined with parchment paper.
4. **Prepare Filling:** Toss the sliced pears with granulated sugar, vanilla extract, and cinnamon. Arrange the pear slices over the dough, leaving a 2-inch border. Sprinkle almond flour over the pears.
5. **Fold and Bake:** Fold the edges of the dough over the pears, pleating as needed. Sprinkle the sliced almonds over the filling. Bake for 35-40 minutes, or until the crust is golden and the pears are tender.
6. **Serve:** Let the tart cool slightly before dusting with powdered sugar, if desired. Serve warm or at room temperature.

Chef's Note:

This Rustic Pear and Almond Tart combines the sweet, delicate flavor of pears with the nutty richness of almonds, all encased in a flaky, buttery crust. The beauty of this tart lies in its simplicity and the rustic charm of its free-form shape. It's a versatile dessert that's perfect for any season and can be made with various fruits depending on what's in season. The almond flour not only adds flavor but also helps to absorb some of the juices from the pears, preventing the crust from becoming soggy. This tart is a delightful way to end a meal or to accompany afternoon tea, offering a balance of flavors and textures that are sure to please.

Thank You

As we reach the final page of our culinary journey, I hope this collection of recipes has inspired you, ignited your passion for cooking, and brought joy to your table.

Whether it was through the simple pleasure of crafting a homemade meal, the excitement of trying a new dish, or the warmth of sharing food with loved ones, my wish is that these pages have added a sprinkle of happiness to your life. Remember, cooking is not just about following recipes—it's about creating memories, experimenting with flavors, and most importantly, cooking with love.

Thank you for inviting me into your kitchen. Here's to many more delicious adventures together.
Bon appétit!

www.ingramcontent.com/pod-product-compliance
Lightning Source LLC
Chambersburg PA
CBHW081115080526
44587CB00021B/3611